The Silence,

The Series,

&

The Season of Sungwoo

by Chris Kamler

Foreword by Rany Jazayerli

Produced in association with Page 3 Network
Platte City, Missouri

Printed by The Covington Group

Cover art and illustrations by Jason Ulitschan

Manufactured in the United States of America

ISBN: 978-1495139833

To Kara, Brett, Andrew, Mom, and Dad

Preface

The past four months of my life have changed me forever. The experience of meeting Sungwoo, taking him around town, the Royals winning and making it to the World Series and losing with a runner only 90 feet away has changed me forever.

I needed to write about it.

I have to admit right off the bat (my first but not last inadvertent baseball pun) that I'm not a big book reader. I read books on the toilet so I've tried to keep most of my chapters short in case you're like me.

For those of you who know me only from Twitter as @TheFakeNed, this will probably be more serious than you thought. For those of you who know me from my day job or from weekly columns I've written for *The Platte County* [MO] *Landmark*, this will probably be much goofier than you thought. For those of you who don't know me at all, this will probably seem like an extremely improbable series of events.

It was.

Chris Kamler
December 2014
@ChrisKamler

Table of Contents

Foreword **by Rany Jazayerli**

I never saw it coming. And if you say you did, you're probably lying.

The 2014 season opened the way the previous 28 seasons had unfolded for the Kansas City Royals: with disappointment followed closely by apathy. A generation of hopelessness and haplessness showed no signs of abating. If anything, the 2014 Royals were more disappointing than their predecessors, because this was the season that the franchise had pointed to for years as the one they were building towards.

The Royals had been so bad for so long that it was actually difficult for me, as a Royals fan, to conceive of a world in which my team *wasn't* bad. Being a Royals fan was like how I imagine it is to be tone-deaf: having a condition that, while not fatal or debilitating, is *annoying*, because you live with the knowledge that there are some life experiences that you were destined to never know.

Little changed through the first half of the 2014 season to alter that perception. The Royals were in last place in early June, and after an out-of-nowhere ten-game winning streak put them in first place two weeks later, they handled their sudden success about as well as your average teenage Disney TV star. On July 21st, the Royals lost their fourth straight game after the All-Star Break, falling to 48–50, in fourth place in the AL Central.

Three months later to the day, they hosted the first game of the World Series.

This book is the story of what happened. This book tells the story of a franchise that for two decades was known for being synonymous with losing if it was known at all, an organization that more than halfway through the 2014 season looked like it had once again wasted a years-long rebuilding process, a team that became the biggest story in American sports for a solid month and the greatest story in Kansas City sports in a generation.

But this book doesn't tell the story from the perspective of breaking down what happened on the field, the trades that were made, the players who were brought up from the minor leagues, general manager Dayton Moore's tactics and manager Ned Yost's strategy. Those were all important and integral parts of what made the 2014 Royals the champions of the American League. But that's not the main thrust* of the story you'll read about in these pages, because this isn't just the story of a team that learned how to win. This is the story of a fan base that learned how to believe again. This is the story of a fan base that learned how to trust that good things could happen to them. This is the story of a fan base that learned how to fall in love with its team.

*Stop giggling, Chris.

I know that's what this story is about because I lived that story — I was that fan. And when the Royals hit their lowest points during the 2014 season, getting swept by the Astros at home in May, getting swept by the Red Sox coming out of the All-Star Break in July, I'm not ashamed to admit that – I stopped believing myself. I had been a fan of the Royals for the entirety of their 29 year postseason drought, the longest active playoff drought in American sports. I had been analyzing and writing about the Royals in various capacities for over 20 years. And I had reached the point where I no longer cared if they won or lost. I just wanted them to pick a side: either win, and justify all the time and money and effort I had invested in the team all these years, or lose mightily and be forced to blow everything up and start over. What I *didn't* want was the metronomic mediocrity of winning and losing in equal measure, finishing near .500 with neither a playoff spot nor a mandate to push the reset button on the franchise. That's exactly what we were getting in late July. I had become a jaded, dare I say bitter, fan.

And that's when the magic happened.

I've known Chris Kamler for several years, the way many of you knew him, as the avatar he plays on Twitter under the name @The-FakeNed: a fat, misanthropic, caustically funny class clown who is always there with a fart joke at the most inappropriate time. But in 2014, I got to know the real Chris, and it turns out I misjudged him completely. Granted, he is fat. And true, he's a bit of a clown. And boy howdy does he like fart jokes.

But he's anything but a misanthrope. It turns out that Chris loves people. He loves them and wants them to be happy. He loves his fellow Royals fans and he loves Kansas City. And I'm convinced that if Chris wasn't the kind of person who would roll out the red carpet to a stranger from South Korea for no other reason than that's what Midwesterners do when a guest arrives, the magic doesn't happen. The 2014 Royals don't happen.

Most Royals fans – hell, most baseball fans – know that the story of the 2014 Royals can't be told without telling the story of Lee Sungwoo. But what very few fans know is that the story of Sungwoo wouldn't have been possible were it not for the guy who wrote the book you are holding. It was Chris who interviewed Sungwoo for his website a few years ago because he was fascinated that a South Korean with no ties to Kansas City could become a Royals fan. It was Chris who even then was inviting — no, insisting that Sungwoo come to Kansas City to see the Royals play someday.

It was Chris to whom Sungwoo confided in June that he had finally arranged that long-awaited trip. And it was Chris who, with the relentless focus of a social media veteran, spread the word that a Royals fan hailing all the way from South Korea was coming to Kansas City to see the Royals play for the first time, and the Royals had even arranged (with some prodding from Chris himself) to let him throw out the first pitch at a game, and it sure would be swell if the city would open up its arms to its new visitor.

What happened after that…well, I'll let Chris tell you what happened after that. But when Sungwoo landed at KCI on a Tuesday afternoon in early August and was met by camera crews from four different local TV stations, I texted Chris:

This is cheesy and corny and condescending to say and I will kill you if you disclose this to anyone, but I'm so proud of what you've done. More to the point, I'm proud to be a Royals fan right now, and that's such a rare feeling. Thank you for that.

I didn't know the half of it.

If that had been the entire story right there, it would have been enough. For the first time in years, I was proud to be a Royals fan, and it had nothing to do with how the Royals actually played on the field. But the story, both for Sungwoo and the Royals, had just begun, and I never saw it coming.

Not Sungwoo becoming a household name, first in Kansas City and then across the nation. Not the winning streak that culminated with Sungwoo holding the blue "W" aloft when the Royals moved into first place a week after he arrived. Not the back-and-forth fight for the division with the Detroit Tigers the rest of August and September. Not sitting behind the dugout with hundreds of other Royals fans in Chicago on the final Friday of the season when they clinched their first playoff spot in a generation. Not opening the playoffs with the greatest game I've ever had the privilege to witness in person — with Chris by my side. And certainly not a chance to finally meet Sungwoo myself when he returned to Kansas City *for the freaking World Series.*

This is a story about a baseball team, but this is also a story about baseball fans. This is a story of sports, but this is also a story of why we love sports so much: not because our teams win or lose, but because — win or lose — our teams bring us together. This is a story about community, and about how in 2014 communities are no longer bound by geography or race or class or even language. Communities can be built simply on a shared love of 25 guys all wearing the same-colored pajama pants.

This is a story about how community brings people together. I knew the power of the Royals community to embrace its own before Sungwoo ever arrived in Kansas City, because I myself have been the beneficiary of that community. I've never lived in Kansas City, and have spent the last 20 years living first in Detroit and then Chicago, and yet I think of Kansas City as my second home. My family doesn't live in Kansas City, but my people do. Chris Kamler is one of those people.

If you know this story, I hope this book helps you to relive it in all its improbable glory. If you don't know this story, you're in for a treat. But not nearly the treat it was for those of us blessed enough to live it.

It's a story I can't wait to tell my grandchildren one day. And who better to tell you that story than the guy who, like a mad alchemist playing with forces he didn't fully understand, started the chain reaction that made it all happen?

The answer is no one. No one is better. Enjoy.

Rany Jazayerli
December, 2014
Co-founder, *Baseball Prospectus*
Grantland.com
@Jazayerli

Chapter 1
The Silence

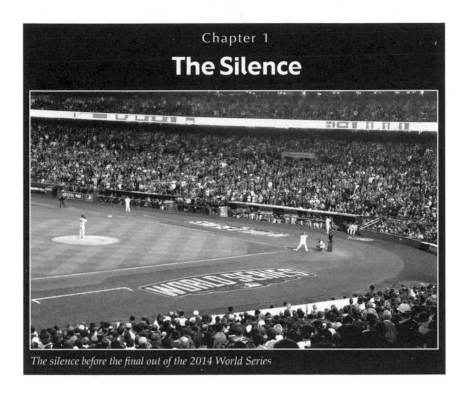

The silence before the final out of the 2014 World Series

Silence.

The absolute absence of noise as if a vacuum has sucked away all of the oxygen from everyone's lungs. It happens all the time in baseball just after the loud crack of the bat and right before the reaction of the crowd. If you listen for it, you'll hear absolute silence.

Pitch up in his eyes. The book on him was out and we all knew it was coming. Salvy couldn't avoid swinging at anything up in his eyes. Yet, the giant man-child Salvador "Salvy" Perez swung anyway. Minutes away from being named the World Series Most Valuable Player, Madison Bumgarner fired the high cheese high above the strike zone. Persecuted in baseball purgatory yet remaining as spectacular as ever, the outfield fountains of Kauffman Stadium and waving towels of the people of Kansas City provided the backdrop.

CRACK. <silence>

So here I am among 40,000 of my closest friends in the most improbable of locations — Kansas City — in the most improbable of settings — the bottom of the ninth inning of Game 7 of the World Series — listening to silence.

I'd only heard silence like that once before. Two years ago. It was there. The same absence of sound. Absolute. Black. Silence.

There are moments in life that you'll absolutely never forget and I've somehow seen hundreds of them just over the past year. This is a story of the late summer of 2014 — when it all seemed to turn around for Kansas City — when a man from South Korea decided to take a leap and cross the biggest item off his bucket list. It's also a story about social media and the power of community. It's a story about a father and a son. It's a story about a fart joke-telling social pariah Forrest Gump'ing his way into the narrative. It's a story about baseball and my hometown. But, as all good baseball stories have to start, I need to first tell you a story about surfing. And that story starts with the moment of silence.

The moment that changed everything. And yet, I long for it to go back to when nothing had changed. That moment of silence will stay with me forever. The complete absence of any sound and possibly the last moment I would have feeling in my limbs. Everything was about to change, and it all starts with this total and absolute moment of silence.

It's the silence I'll remember the most.

Chapter 2

The Laughter

Huntington Beach, California - the morning of the accident

I'd never laughed so hard. And this was AFTER the accident. This was after I had spent the first day laughing and drinking and carrying on. After I had been made young again by spending a "guy's weekend" in 2012 with my bros in sunny Huntington Beach, California.

"This is what we do now, fly to California for the weekend," my friend Brett, an author and former small town mayor, kept saying. "This is what we do. Just fly to the coast for the weekend." He meant it facetiously, yet quite literally, we were flying out to Cali from Kansas City for a few days for a little rest and relaxation, but mostly to laugh. And to feel young.

Four friends who had grown 25 years. Grown apart. Grown up. This was a weekend to reconnect. Almost immediately, the roles fit back together like puzzle pieces that had been in different corners of a house. There was the intellectual, slightly hippie vibe of Brett.

3

The laid-back, Steve Jobsian "mountain climber" in Phil, a guy who turns everything he touches to gold. And then my friend Wheezy, the mother hen of the group. (And I say this in a good way.) The protector. He had seen for years what had been happening to our little clique, how we had talked less and less and generally slowed down. This was the chance to fix that. Or at least to slow down the gentle erosion that time can cause on friendships. Wives, kids, e-mails — there would be very few of these over the weekend, just some drinking, some goofing around and, oh yes, lots of laughter, thanks to his generous gift of flying us all out to the coast for the weekend.

Then there was my role in the group. The jester. It's a role that I slipped back into like an old baseball mitt you'd find in the garage. Joking, jabbing, giving shit. That's MY role. And it was just as important as the other three.

Back in 1988, our little high school group watched a movie featuring a young Emilio Estevez. It's name... *Young Guns*. It was about a group of outlaws patrolling the wild, wild west. Our group's nickname in high school was "The Dirty Underwear Gang" because the Young Guns posse was called "The Dirty Underwear Gang out of Liberty, Missouri." It was one of those names that just stuck because of its sheer stupidity, and yet it fit us perfectly. Well, the DUG had certainly aged, but once we stepped off the plane, the ages immediately rolled back and we were 18 again — with less hair. But I digress.

Day one was about great food, some booze and watching the beauty of a California sunset beyond the palm trees and the ocean. Day two was all about activities. Frankly, I'd have been fine just being hungover until around noon when the drinking would've started back up. Lather, rinse, repeat. But I was the couch potato hanging with three accomplished mountain-climbing, paragliding, hiking, biking, wake-up-before-noon-on-Saturday over-achievers.

My accident was just that, a true accident. It was due to a combination of location, lack of awareness and just dumb luck.

Huntington Beach is a prime location for well-conditioned surfers. We saw many of them that morning as we walked the pier. It is also, however, a keen place for danger because of the confusing surf breaks present there. The best place to surf a break is the farthest break out, where the waves are the highest and the most "pure." That is, the energy is traveling in one direction, towards the shore. In Huntington, there are two and sometimes three breaks because of the way the shore blocks that energy. It was my first time bodysurfing and I was very nervous about it.

"If you guys can find a body suit for my fat ass, I'm in," I told them.

We took baby steps and before I knew it, I was having the time of my life. Bodysurfing the powerful ocean waves was exhilarating. It seemed so simple and silly to have water pushing me forward, but I was hooked. It was just what I needed that weekend — to be free. To fly.

Luck is defined as "a force that brings good fortune or adversity," and it is that force, that energy that I had been playing with for an hour and a half. But I was doing it on the second break on crashing waves, riding the frothing foam, the chaos, all the way into shore. And, if I do say so myself, I was doing pretty well.

Little did I know, at sunset on Huntington Beach, the sea turns angrier.

The waves grew. And soon we lost track of Phil. Captain America. Had to go out to the furthest breakers and took the "rip tide" further down the beach. So the three of us left the water to go check on him. We eventually found him, apparently after he didn't find a mountain to climb or a baby to save, and we all huddled back up to take stock of the surfing so far and catch our breath.

Wheezy laid his surfboard down on the beach and sat down on it. Next to him sat Phil. Brett flanked them on his boogie board to their left and I sat down on my board to their right. It was a postcard moment. The sun had just started to go down in the west, dipping below the horizon.

For a number of minutes, we didn't say anything and just looked out upon the majesty of where we were. Of what we were seeing. We had felt that power, that energy and we had, for just a few minutes, been able to ride that force. Our conversation then reopened and we talked boastfully about the waves we had "shredded" and the ones we didn't catch.

It was a conversation between four lifelong friends whose lives were about to be changed.

It was clear that we weren't done surfing yet. We had to go back out there and shred more.

I never really got surfing before. I get surfing now. You are riding the wind. You are pushing your luck.

The four of us got up, and I headed into the water first, followed by my guys. The guy who had to be convinced to squeeze into a black bodysuit to surf was now leading the guys back into the water.

I had gotten about 15 feet into the ocean when I noticed that the place we entered the beach was different. We later labeled it "meaner." The waves were a little bit higher and as I hit about the 20-foot mark, I saw a whitecap just starting to form. This matched the same parameters of whitecaps I caught earlier in the day, the only difference was that I was closer to shore. I was still standing with the water up to my chest. I was standing on "the inside." Which is what accomplished surfers call the place too shallow to surf. (A fun, timely fact I learned from the ambulance driver as he was speeding me to an emergency room.)

Plus, the afternoon sun adds to the explosiveness of wave energy.

I turned to catch the wave and surf the short 20 feet back to shore.

I turned to my right and jumped and spun.

Everything was different. Everything was wrong.

Instead of being pushed horizontally at my butt and back, I felt a very powerful energy underneath my feet pushing up, vertically. Instead of setting up at an inclined angle, I had somehow gotten into a declined angle, like I was teetering head-first down a playground slide. Pointing down. Pointing the wrong way. Straight down.

It is at this moment that things slowed way down. I can tell you microsecond by microsecond what happened next. Not because the energy was any slower, if anything it was faster. I can tell you it was the most real moment of my life.

Pitched downward, the energy did not dissipate. Rather, it pushed me down 5 feet — down the playground slide into the ocean floor. My face plowed into the gritty ground with a dull thud and I was enveloped in silence. Only that moment was followed by even more force, even more power. Then pressure. Then pain. The ocean's relentless surge drove my face deeper into the sandy bottom. I felt the skin on my face start to split open and the wet grains of sand touching me. The power bent me backwards, with my feet surging forward as my face stayed buried in the sand. I imagine I looked like a spandex-wearing black Michelin Man bent backward into a really poorly shaped "C" as the energy continued to push my body, blocked only by my face in the sand.

I couldn't feel anything. I couldn't breathe. I was underwater. I'm pretty sure I was face down. All of these specific thoughts popped into my brain in nanoseconds.

Then I thought about dying.

I knew I had a serious problem. I couldn't move my feet. I couldn't move my hands. I was still underwater. I was completely calm, and yet, I was completely unable to do anything.

I had met luck. And I had met it, quite literally, head on.

The thing about luck, though, is that it only encapsulates an event. Something with a beginning and an end. This event only lasted a moment, but that meant another moment had to come next.

The next moments were kinder, the energy wave passed by me, the boogie board which was providing much of the resistance finally flew away from my body and I somehow (and I honestly don't know how) flipped face up in the water.

I took a quick inventory of what was working. Hands? No. Feet? No. But my neck was working and I was close enough to the surface to lift my head out of the water. At that point, luck started to run my way because my friends that I had sat so close to on the beach just moments before were still very close to me. Five minutes later and they would've been 50 feet away and I would've easily drowned.

I turned my head to the left and found Wheezy's eyes. The first "help" didn't come out, but I kept his gaze. The second "help" wasn't much louder because I still wasn't breathing, but it was audible. Brett sprinted over to me and yelled, "He's bleeding," and he did his best to stabilize my neck between crashing waves.

"I can't move anything. I can't move anything. I'm sorry. I'm so sorry."

"Let's get him out of the water."

The fortune of nearly killing myself "on the inside" also meant they only had to drag me about ten feet to shore.

"Be careful, I'm pretty sure I hurt my neck real bad."

Fortune took away and also gave that day. Had Phil not almost gotten lost, we might've just left after our first tussle with the sea. Had the power of the wave been just a little bit stronger, my neck could've easily snapped.

The laughter I referred to is what happened AFTER the accident. Oh, sure, the day before we made jokes, talked about how we'd all look "fly" in the hip-hop clothes of the store we walked through. But the laughter was never deeper, never fuller than when the guys started making jokes in the back of the ambulance. IN THE BACK OF THE AMBULANCE.

As my body was in shock and trembling from the absolute terror of possibly being paralyzed, the guys were cracking wise. There was a "dirty underwear" crack that I chuckled at. There was a crack about not getting back my deposit on the body suit that I had rented just two hours prior. And then, there was the crack in the ambulance about me doing pretty good for my first time out — except for, yanno, the paralysis.

The ambulance driver asked me where I was from. When I told him Kansas City, he said, "Oh, we get a lot of Midwesterners in this ambulance." Ordinarily, these cracks might seem out of sorts or insensitive, but they were absolutely vital to my not completely losing it at that moment in time. My role was the jokester, so that's what needed to be filled to make the group whole. The group was whole. The group was a complete unit. Jokes would fill the seams. And once the tension was slightly lessened, once the situation went from life-threatening to merely serious, that's when the shit REALLY started to fly.

In the ER we were merciless to the nurses. Partly because it was clearly a coping mechanism, and partly because the nurses were down with it and giving it back as hard as we were giving it to them. We were just pestering these poor girls trying to insert IV fluids or take a blood pressure. And whatever pain meds they gave me weren't helping because I started in on them, too.

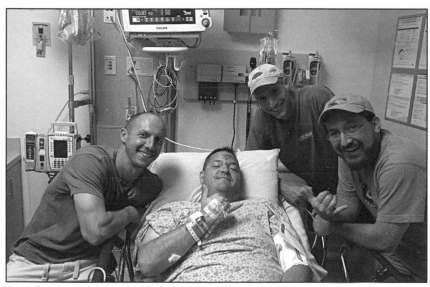

I'm still waiting on the results of my pregnancy test.

Wheezy reminded me that being strapped to a backboard with a C-collar taped to your head is the perfect time for a "friend" to hit you in the junk. At one point I asked a nurse if my pregnancy test had come back. (It hadn't.)

The ultimate moment of hilarity was when they began to cut off the rest of my lycra body suit. Well, there's no dignity when a nurse is standing at your toes with scissors and you hear the first cut inches away from your leg. As she got to my knee, I told her, "now, I have trunks on underneath these, don't cut my trunks." As if they were made of gold leaf and not $7 from Wal-Mart. The nurse nodded and kept carefully cutting the fabric above my knee. Then she got to my lower thigh. No swim trunks. Then she got to my mid thigh. No swim trunks. It wasn't until she got nearly to the top of my thigh that we found my supposedly "baggy" swim trunks. That were tucked neatly in whatever crevice I had left in my crotch. The guys let me have it. When all you have left is dignity, it's hilarious when it is ripped from you. Or rather pulled from you. With both hands.

The shock that my body was going through — the trembling — the tear down my cheek — was all completely offset by the guys and the laughing. You really had to be there to understand how totally okay all of this was. Because if you were just walking by the ER room, you'd probably have thought how completely inappropriate all of this was.

I was whole. I was complete. I was going to be okay.

It was because of laughter.

Chapter 3

The Talisman, The Fake, and The King

"Twitter Celebs" Lee Sungwoo and Jimmy Faseler celebrating a Royals victory

Lee Sungwoo is now a household name in the kitchens and sports bars of Kansas City. Folks who don't even follow baseball or the Royals know the story of the lifelong Royals fan who flew across the globe to attend his first Royals game in person. It was picked up across the country and the world. Local news, ABC News, the *New York Times*, SBS, MBC Sports in Korea and even the BBC in England all told the tale of the "superfan" Sungwoo. To me, he is much more than a superfan, but we'll get to that.

In a nutshell, 20 years ago Lee wanted to learn English to improve his chances at a great job in South Korea. He started following the Armed Forces Network, often listening to baseball games because they provided a great version of the language called "baseball English." You'll often hear Japanese players come to America and learn baseball terms first (and more than a few iterations of the word "fuck").

But instead of just learning English, he also fell in love with the game of baseball and the nuance that the pace of the game provided.

He learned the language, but also the unspoken language of pitch outs and reading pitchers to get a jump on a stolen base. He also chose "his" team wisely.

Sungwoo and his younger brother Lee SungJin both began to follow the Royals with Sungwoo being the more positive and SungJin being the more cynical. Sungwoo likened it to Rob Neyer and Rany Jazayerli's "Rob and Rany on the Royals" website that often featured point/counterpoint arguments about the future of the Royals franchise.

Sungwoo's fandom extended well past his humble apartment with his wife in South Korea. As his love of baseball grew, so did his voice in the electronic fan community of the late 1990s and early 2000s when BBSs and message boards were small collections of fans on the relatively young Information Superhighway.

KoreanFan_KC was born.

As is so often the case in Royals fandom, however, following this team closely usually ends each year in frustration, aggravation and early elimination from any hopes of the playoffs. Sungwoo's positivity stood out even back when I started writing about the Royals.

Either the snark never translated to Sungwoo, or his eternal optimism overshadowed it. An early Internet bulletin board called Royals Corner soon evolved with the Internet and gave way to blogs and now Twitter, but through the format changes, KoreanFan_KC remained a beacon of positive fandom on display.

Sungwoo admits he doesn't recall the exact moment the Royals became *his* team, but it was in the late 1990s that he recalls making a bucket list item that would eventually find the club and his mojo colliding 15 years later.

===============

In 1999, Jeff King was finishing the final year of his career with the Royals. He was a ten-year veteran of Major League Baseball, playing for the Pittsburgh Pirates from 1989-1996. He was a first-round draft pick for Pittsburgh and was a key to three division championships with the Pirates of the early 1990s that featured Barry Bonds and Bobby Bonilla.

But by the time he reached Kansas City, as was the case with a lot of players in the 1990s and 2000s, King's career was on a downward trajectory, and he landed on a team that was among the worst in baseball. Furthermore, he was traded for fan favorite Joe Randa (called "the Joker" because of his always present smile), so Royals fans were already skittish on his arrival.

This fueled the fire on message boards and chat rooms, which were sparsely attended by a small, albeit consistent, group of fans.

King fought off back problems through his career and retired a couple of weeks into the 1999 season one day after he became fully vested in the MLB pension program. The great *Kansas City Star* columnist and national baseball writer Joe Posnanski wrote about King,

> *Best I could tell, Jeff King did not like playing baseball. I'm not kidding about how much he disliked the game. His manager in Kansas City, Tony Muser, used to tell a story about how he heard King moaning one day about the National Anthem. Muser, a former Marine, was shocked but King explained: "Every time they play this song, I have a bad day." He generally looked like he would rather be anyplace else on earth.*
>
> *On May 21, 1999 Jeff King suddenly and shockingly retired. He seemed healthy, and he seemed to be having a reasonably successful year — he was on a little six-game hitting streak at the time. It didn't make a lot of sense ... unless you realized how much he despised playing professional baseball. He couldn't wait to get out. Later someone told me that he had, only the day before he retired, secured enough service time to guarantee his MLB pension. With that, he went off to a ranch in Wyoming or some such place.*

During his career with the Royals, he hit only 55 homers and only 26 of those came in the vast expanse of Kauffman Stadium — a notoriously difficult place to hit homers. But one of those 26 homers changed the life of Lee Sungwoo. "I saw Jeff King hit a homer at The

K. I saw the fireworks going off and the fans cheering, and I said, this was a place I want to see."

So thank you, Jeff King because you brought us the talisman that would forever change the course of the 2014 Royals season and the city of Kansas City.

I began to know Sungwoo through Twitter during the 2012 season, and he also developed relationships with a number of fans and even players. Danny Duffy, a rookie pitcher for the Royals, famously invited him to Kansas City on his dime.

The 2012 season was particularly heartbreaking in the pantheon of heartbreaking Royals seasons. Moody yet brilliant Zack Greinke had signed as a free agent with the Brewers, then traded to the Angels prior to the season. The team played host to the 2012 All-Star Game, yet finished with 90 losses — good for third in the American League Central. Young talent in Eric Hosmer and Mike Moustakas had not developed and Billy Butler and Alex Gordon weren't pulling their weight. (Stop me if you've heard this before.)

Even through the pain and suffering of being a Royals fan online, Sungwoo always stood out above the fray to make us all feel better about any given situation.

===============

In addition to my close circle of real-life friends, I also counted 12,234 others among my "Fake" life friends on Twitter — although that title is completely misleading in many ways.

Fake Ned was a character I made up the night former Kansas City Royals manager Trey Hillman was fired as the manager of the club. His successor was a perceived bumbling, grumpy baseball man who was fired with two weeks to go in a pennant race in Milwaukee — Ned Yost.

To me, Yost typified only the latest in a long line of leaders destined to keep my favorite baseball team wallowing in the basement of the American League. The seat may stay the same, but the butts (and the buttholes) that occupy it are simply paper dolls in a failing franchise.

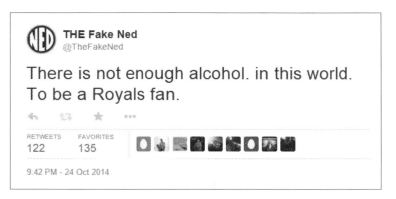

There was Buddy Bell, former All-Star catcher who during his tenure as manager of the club famously said, "I never say it can't get worse."

There was Tony Peña, another former All-Star who jumped into a shower in full uniform as a show of leadership to a team in the middle of a losing streak.

Hillman was but the latest casualty. The only recognizable thing I can remember him doing was putting out an album of Christmas songs while he was managing in Japan. When he got the Royals job, he went on the radio with Sports Radio 810 WHB's Kevin Kietzman and they played part of it for Hillman. The rest of his managerial career was, um, uneventful.

Yost was coming off the ultimate showing of a lack of confidence in Milwaukee — being fired as the team was clinging to a postseason berth. "Nervous Ned" he was called, and in the world of Twitter, that meant it was open season.

I joined Twitter in 2010 like many of us did: very cautiously. The medium takes some getting used to, but the short sentence structure, the limit of 140 characters, and the ability to throw out a thought and then have it basically disappear all drew me in.

It was a way to verbalize much of the inner dialogue we all have — most of mine featuring fart jokes and talk of boobs.

Some of my favorite accounts to follow were "parody" accounts. There was a great one back then of Steve Jobs, the late founder of

Apple. The template for the parody account was to stay in character as a cartoonish version of the person you were parodying

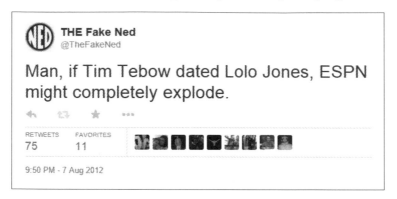

THE Fake Ned
@TheFakeNed

Man, if Tim Tebow dated Lolo Jones, ESPN might completely explode.

RETWEETS   FAVORITES
75   11

9:50 PM - 7 Aug 2012

@FakeSteveJobs, for instance, would poetically go on about how one could make the iToilet. Along with the Jobs account, thousands of others have popped up, including those in the sports world — the two most famous in the Midwest being @DanBeebe and @FauxPelini. Beebe was the former commissioner of the Big 12 conference that saw Nebraska, Colorado, Missouri and Texas A&M all leave the conference under his watch. The parody account is a hyper dickish version of Beebe making fun of the dissenting teams as well as the conference that ultimately pushed him out.

Faux Pelini is just the best thing ever. Bo Pelini was the fiery head coach of the Nebraska Cornhuskers football team until late 2014. His appearance is often that of a dull oak tree who screams a lot, and his parody Twitter account is one part dumb football jock and one part college football cynic. Saturday Night Live in its prime never provided satire the way Faux Pelini does.

Having learned Twitter for about a year, and thinking I was a pretty funny guy, I created a @NotTreyHillman account to try my hand at the medium.

Hillman was so dull and inept as manager, however, the account never really was able to satire much of his actions. He was fired only a few weeks later and @FakeNedYost was born.

Fake Ned Yost tweeted in character for the first couple of months and mostly during live baseball games when Royals fans were most active on Twitter. If Yost came out of the dugout and argued with an umpire, Fake Ned would tweet something like, "That guy's breath smelled like onions and Pepto Bismol." If the team was flying to Cleveland for a road trip, Fake Ned would riff on ways Kansas City is better than Cleveland. "Not being Cleveland" was high on the list.

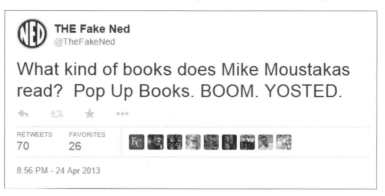

But I was never very good at staying in character. Fake Ned evolved quickly into just being my account with a thin veil of anonymity that then allowed me to act with no filter. You don't know how freeing it is to be able to tell people you disagree with that they're a stupid son of a bitch, and Fake Ned allowed me that veil

So Fake Ned ended up just being a louder, crankier, more vulgar version of myself and tweeted during baseball games, football games, the Oscars, the Country Music Awards, Tuesday, Sunday night — anywhere that snark, vulgarity and drunkenness were appropriate to be put on display.

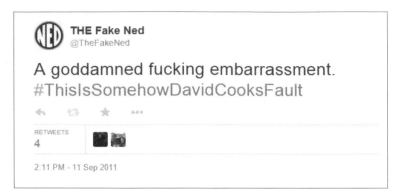

The avenue, however, became a playground for me. It is the best format for which I think, often rudely, in short, direct, encapsulated thoughts. Also, there are boobs on there sometimes, which is neat.

The account became fairly popular in 2012, getting several thousand followers, and it was even the subject of a newspaper article in *The Kansas City Star's* Ink Magazine.

> You might not know Chris Kamler. But if you're a Kansas City sports fans, one of the diehards, there's a decent chance you know Kamler's crass alter ego: @FakeNedYost, or more recently, @TheFakeNed — an homage to real Royals manager Ned Yost.

Today, Fake Ned is among the most heavily followed fan accounts in Kansas City. It was really never designed to be a popular account. It was just an outlet for a frustrated fan who saw a death spiral of a baseball team, but it struck a chord with many. And that popularity has now evolved into the community that is Royals Twitter.

At its heart, however, Fake Ned is just a tortured fan of his hometown baseball team. The root of all of the fart jokes and all of the cursing and even that one time I put on a blue bra — all of that was based out of love. Love for George and Frank and Mr. K and Hos and Moose and even Ned and Dayton. Okay, maybe the bra thing was just a drunken prank.

But neither Fake Ned, nor Sungwoo, nor even Jeff King could've predicted what awaited in 2014.

THE Fake Ned @TheFakeNed   02 May

Okay. I'm bought in. This is me buying in. Break my heart, you bastards. I give it to you freely. #Royals #ComeToPlay

Rany Jazayerli
@jazayerli

@TheFakeNed DON'T DO IT FAKE NED!! YOU'RE MAKING A BIG MISTAKE!! YOU HAVE SO MUCH LIFE AHEAD OF YOU!!

10:31 PM - 1 May 2013

6 FAVORITES

Chapter 4

The Team, The Transition, and The Trade

Royals owner David Glass and Royals General Manager Dayton Moore at the 2014 preseason Fan Fest

Prior to 2014, being a fan of the Kansas City Royals was an exercise in Charlie Brownastics. Let me explain. The famous Peanuts cartoon with Lucy and Snoopy and Charlie Brown featured a recurring gag whereby Lucy would hold a football for Charlie Brown to kick. Charlie Brown would charge to the football only to have Lucy yank it away at the last minute. That's not the gag though.

The gag is that it happens every time. Charlie Brown KNOWS that it's going to happen every time, but is somehow convinced by Lucy that it won't this time. Lucy has no intention of ever letting Charlie Brown kick the football. Ever. In a million years. That's what being a Royals fan is like.

My fandom began through the glory years of the 1970s and 1980s. I cried when Chris Chambliss hit the home run to defeat the Royals in the 1976 American League Championship Series, and at the ripe old age of 13, my cousin and I bought face value, standing-room-only tickets for Game 7 of the 1985 World Series. So believe me when I tell you, I've seen the highs and lows.

But the lows only got lower after that crisp October night in 1985. The manager of that team, Dick Howser, died following the next season due to a brain tumor. The team signed risky free agents with one of the largest payrolls in baseball in the late 1980s only to have the financial landscape of baseball change due to labor strife in the 1990s.

Jump to May 23, 1993. A dying Ewing Kauffman made his final appearance at Royals Stadium, a facility that would be renamed in his honor a month later and a month after that, he would be gone. "Mr. K" stepped onto the pristine manicured George Toma masterpiece and waved goodbye to the franchise that he loved. Behind the scenes, the man who brought Major League Baseball back to Kansas City after the Athletics snuck out the back door, the man who refused to trade George Brett, the man who held stern fatherly discussions with players following a drug scandal and the man who brought a championship to the Heartland — Mr. Kauffman was putting into place a complicated, unorthodox and very specific transfer of power plan that would ultimately doom the franchise for decades.

In the early 1960s, Ewing Kauffman was becoming a self-made millionaire. His method of success was pharmaceuticals and an aggressive business philosophy with a twinkle in his eye. Kansas City was the home of the Athletics and the miserly owner Charlie Finley. When Finley packed up his "swingin' A's" and headed to Oakland to win three consecutive World Championships, Kansas City was left without a professional baseball franchise.

Kauffman stepped up, lobbied Major League Baseball and promised his own money to buy an expansion team. The Kansas City Royals began in 1969 and the next two decades were beyond successful, culminating with a 1985 World Series Championship, capping off a decade of six playoff appearances and two World Series appearances.

Every Royals fan knows this story. They've heard the tales of Kauffman's tenacious management style and fatherly "dressing down" sessions with players. He was aggressive in contract negotiations but was the proudest Royals fan when they won.

I recall going to games with my dad and looking up at the Kauffmans' suite on the Club Level of Royals Stadium. Nearly every time, he would be sitting there, in a blue blazer, often with the window open waving back at fans. In my child-like brain, I wondered if he was some sort of king or monarch of Kansas City. In a small way, he was.

What Mr. K could not foresee was the changes coming to the game of baseball in the 1990s and 2000s. His dying wish, that baseball remain in Kansas City, actually set into motion a guarantee that subpar baseball would continue indefinitely in Kansas City. Kauffman "donated" his franchise to a charitable trust, the Greater Kansas City Community Foundation, where it would stay under the stewardship of a five-person Board of Directors led by Wal-Mart chairman David Glass.

Mr. Kauffman donated the team to a committee. A committee that ultimately ended up being impotent when it came to spending money and working toward the future. Labor unrest through the 1990s, small and large market baseball, the rise of the steroid era and the age of technology all blossomed around the ownership "group" of the Royals until 2000 when MLB accepted a $96 million bid for the Royals by David Glass. (MLB took the lower of two bids as Miles Prentice reportedly offered $117 million and was rejected by MLB twice.)

The only stipulation in the sale of the franchise was that it remain in Kansas City.

The stipulation meant that whether or not the team lost money, the team could never leave. Regardless of the economic impact of the region, regardless of the shifting of money to the Johnson County, Kansas side of the state and regardless of the age of television and multi-media contracts, the Kansas City Royals had to stay locked in concrete as the growth and evolution of Major League Baseball went on around it.

The absence of that clause might have very well ended with the Royals leaving Kansas City in the early 2000s or possibly even being contracted. But it also could've meant that the team could've been sold easily and quickly to ownership with actual money to spend and a mentality for winning. We'll never know.

At best, the decision to allow a charitable board of directors to own a franchise was bold and brave; at worst, it was a slow wound in the side of a proud franchise at a terrible time in baseball history where a single, powerful voice could've kept the team above water. Ewing Kauffman is praised as a visionary businessman, a shrewd negotiator and the savior of baseball in Kansas City. His final acts, however, set in motion very nearsighted and, ultimately paralyzing, decades of losing that an extra-inning victory in a Wild Card game in 2014 began to repair — 20 years later.

===============

It was 1994. Ace of Base's "The Sign" was the number 1 music single in America. I was dropping out of college for the first of four times and the Kansas City Royals were in first place and won 26 out of 30 games. This was the same year Lee Sungwoo began following Major League Baseball to learn English.

1994 was the year it all changed for the Royals and the city. 1994 was followed by nothingness. The 1994 MLB work stoppage happened. Manager Hal McRae was fired. Ewing Kauffman had died and a rash of misery heretofore never seen in baseball history fell upon the Kansas City Royals for the next 20 years.

Jeff King happened. Mark and Storm Davis happened. Ken Harvey and Jason Grimsley collided on an infield single. That actually happened. The Kauffman trust — a charitable trust designed to keep the Royals in KC that ended up being a decade-long albatross around the neck of the team in the late 1990s — happened. Yuniesky Betancourt happened — twice. Fireworks were set off after Mark Quinn drew an intentional walk. Hal McRae hit a reporter with a phone in what continues to be one of the top five sports rants of all time according to every list show and website ever. The list goes on for miles.

Kansas City was also slowly drifting away from the Boys in Blue as the Chiefs were in their renaissance decade with Marty Schottenheimer, Derrick Thomas and those great teams of the 1990s. The Chiefs never got to a Super Bowl, but they got a helluva lot further than the land of misfit toys across the parking lot at Truman Sports Complex.

The Pitch, Kansas City's alternative newspaper, put it very well when they described the years that followed the championship season of 1985:

> *In 1985, Royals GM John Schuerholz won a World Series ring. Then it all went wrong. In an effort to obtain one last championship for owner Ewing Kauffman, Schuerholz traded Danny Jackson, later the National League Cy Young winner, for average shortstop Kurt Stillwell. He traded David Cone in 1987, who went on to win eight postseason starts, for catcher Ed Hearn, who started eight games. Schuerholz signed free agents Storm Davis and Mark Davis, who both pitched disastrously here. Kauffman died in 1991 [sic], and Schuerholz, having failed to win another championship for him, moved to the Atlanta Braves. The Braves played in a World Series two years later.*

A strong first half of the 2003 season started to perk up the fanbase and even convinced my wife Kara and me to become season ticket holders for the 2004 season. The 2004 team was picked by many to win the American League Central with offensive weapons including David DeJesus and Joe Randa (on his second tour with the Royals.) Their pitching was expected to compete with names including Jeremy Affeldt, Kevin Appier and a young Zack Greinke, the heir apparent. True to character, though, the '04 team turned out to be one of the worst in baseball history.

Our season ticket package was for every fourth home game — a quarter of the season. And it so happened that due to dumb luck, every time we went to the game, Brian Anderson, who was at the tail end of his career, pitched. We must've seen him pitch 12 times that year. Anderson was awful, posting a 6-12 record in 2004 with a 5.64

ERA. He personified just what a dumpster fire that club was. One step forward for the Royals, 17 steps back.

The strike of 1994 wiped out the last playoff chance the Royals had for another 20 years and there were thousands of decisions and trades and plays and players to be cussed and discussed in that time.

But the epicenter or turning point, depending on how you look at it, of the bitching and moaning world happened on December 10, 2012, when number one draft pick and number one prospect in the Royals farm system, Wil Myers, and top pitching prospect Jake Odorizzi were traded to the Tampa Bay Rays for relief pitcher Wade Davis and starting pitcher "Big Game" James Shields.

This will forever be referred to by Royals fans as "The Trade."

The trade was crushed widely by reporters, bloggers and Royals Twitter (now its own character in this passion play). A national baseball writer for Grantland.com, Rany Jazayerli said at the time, "Let's start here: Wil Myers is not a good prospect. He is not a very good prospect. He is one of the best prospects in baseball, almost certain to be among the top five of every prospect list that is published this offseason." Rany was not pleased that he was now a Tampa Bay Ray and neither were the majority of the national writers who looked at the move as renting a pitcher for two years while destroying the future of the franchise.

I am a tremendous fan of citizen reporters, which is another topic for another day. But one of my favorites who covers the Royals is Michael Engel. He does a weekly podcast and writes in some of the same blogger circles that I do. He and I were talking about "The Trade" the other day and he reminded me that it was in direct contrast to how the '85 Championship team was built. That 1985 team had some of the best pitching in franchise history with Danny Jackson, Dan Quisenberry, Charlie Leibrandt, Buddy Black, and the list goes on, including 1985 World Series MVP Bret Saberhagen (1985's version of Madison Bumgarner).

Engel said that the Royals were simply unable to develop pitching after the early 2000s no matter how hard they tried. "When they did, it didn't coincide with any other success (like Greinke, who was part of the first "The Trade"). The franchise remained doomed post-Mr. K (four top 25 overall pitching prospects of which only Duffy has had success as a Royal), so the Shields trade was the big name guy the Royals had been looking for for a while."

Nobody understood at the time what Shields would bring to a club completely lost in the culture of losing except, maybe, general manager Dayton Moore. Shields was an excellent pitcher with the Tampa Bay Rays, but his leadership was what the Royals wanted. Shields immediately changed the culture from one of Frat House immaturity to one of Frat House maturity. The baseball cliché is that he "taught the team how to be winners," which is bullshit, but he did make winning fun.

He brought in a secret ritual after wins at home that included indoor pyrotechnics and a goofy neon sign of a deer's ass that would be lit after a victory. None of this was designed for the fans — this was only for the players. He carried himself with honor and pitched his ass off in 2013 for the Royals, posting a 13-9 record with a solid (but not extraordinary) 3.19 earned run average (ERA).

But that 2013 season was half of the expected Royals career for James Shields, who only had two years remaining on his contract. And although the team wasn't mathematically eliminated until the final week of the season, a dreadful month of May where the Royals won only eight games caused enough damage to the hull that the season was sunk from that point forward.

Club tent poles like Alex Gordon and Billy Butler had strong years, but not strong enough to overcome the hole they dug in May. The Trade was talked about nearly every day through the offseason as a colossal flop.

Jazayerli said in 2012 that Myers had an 86% chance of being an impact player for a team. Myers won Rookie of the Year honors in his first season with the Rays with a WAR* of 1.9, 13 home runs and a .295 batting average. Oh, and he also made the postseason with

---

WAR stands for Wins Above Replacement and is an amalgam of several statistics. Basically, it is used to compare players to other players. Higher WAR's are good players. Lower WAR's (or negative WAR's) are bad players.

the Rays, who were knocked out in the division round after winning the Wild Card game. While the verdict was not in after only Myers' first season with the Rays (and it's still not in — as of this writing, he has been traded to the San Diego Padres), the challenge has always been measuring the intangible — the "heart" of a team that SABR** followers haven't come up with a formula for yet.

But the Royals stood on the brink — just like in 2003 — that if they could get their act together, avoid a long losing streak, and catch a few breaks, they could avoid 2004. Maybe. Hopefully.

But as a Royals fan, I wouldn't believe it until I saw it with my own eyes. All they needed... was a spark.

** *SABR is the Society for American Baseball Research. Some call them the future of baseball as they can help analyze baseball through statistical analysis, others cynically call them nerds who live in their mother's basement having never played the game.*

Chapter 5

The Committee and The Apple Pie

Members of the Sungwoo Welcoming Committee on a tour of Kauffman Stadium

Going into 2014, hopes were high for the Royals. Those who frequented Royals Twitter or Sports Radio were skeptical... it could still turn into another lost season — the equivalent of Lucy finding a new and creative way to pull the football away from Charlie Brown at the last possible moment.

By June, the Royals were showing some signs of life, but they were only hovering around .500. They had spent some days in first place in the AL Central, but also many days in last place as well. There was certainly no sense of impending magic and chaos, and the fanbase had settled into its yearly routine of ripping every decision, policy, and play by the home nine.

The immediacy of Twitter allows fans to jump to completely irrational and knee-jerk conclusions. It's really pretty entertaining. Offseason moves are immediately projected out 162 games. Injuries are catastrophic and every announcer is the worst if they don't completely knob-slob your team. Twitter is insane on nearly any subject, which makes Royals Twitter an incredibly dysfunctional family.

Imagine 500 of your friends and family members sitting around Thanksgiving dinner with no filter on: Uncle Earl and your drunk cousin Gary and your sister Jenny, who ran off with that guy stocking up on government cheese living in a bunker in Montana. Imagine the conversations. The arguments. The complaining. That's Royals Twitter — only magnified by a billion.

An extremely incomplete listing of topics of complaint by those in the *Twitteratti* included:

- Third baseman Mike Moustakas, whose batting average was below .200;

- Television commentator Rex Hudler, who has been a lightning rod for those who listen to every minute of every game, since 92% of those minutes contain Hudler's hyper-promotive drivel;

- Ned Yost and what #Yosted event would be next to lose a game, whether he would make a substitution, call for a bunt or just sit there picking his nose;

- "Big Game" James Shields looking more like "Big Lame";

- Eric Hosmer and that terrible haircut;

- Fat Billy Butler and how frequently he grounds into double-plays;

- The elimination of... okay this really put it into perspective... the elimination of the traditional sixth inning song of Garth Brooks' "Friends in Low Places" (which Royals Twitter ultimately won, marking the first time Twitter has ever been used for good).

As usual, the @KoreanFan_KC account was a dose of calm in the frustration. On June 9th, the heavens opened up at Kauffman Stadium and threatened the cancellation of that night's game. Sungwoo tweeted from South Korea in the wee hours of the morning of June 10th his time:

SungWoo Lee
@Koreanfan_KC
Sorry for postpone homegame #Royals..
But The K looks so beautiful..."@goldbergkc: As of right now, tarp is on
pic.twitter.com/At6AFGuviG"

5:40 PM - 9 Jun 2014

1 RETWEET

When a fan posted a photograph of the infamous Don Denkinger call in Game 6 of the 1985 World Series, Sungwoo said:

SungWoo Lee
@Koreanfan_KC
Looked batter safe...already passed base, out of pic... #Royals World
Champion ;-P
"@ConradMcGorkin: LOLZ !!! #BFIB pic.twitter.com/p06InNKQCV"

9:31 PM - 5 Jun 2014

1 FAVORITE

(The ;-P emoticon being the wink while sticking out tongue in sarcasm, of course.)

I was fascinated with this single voice amongst what was normally a cesspool of negativity and despair.

From the first time I interviewed Lee Sungwoo, I was a fan. His spirit transcended the time zones and distance, and we became digital pen pals. He also made friendships with a number of other "tweeps," as he likes to call them.

After the 2012 season, my website RamblingMorons.com, which was a longer-form version of my fart-jokes from Twitter, awarded him the "Fan of the Year" award and I implored him to come to Kansas City.

> *RamblingMorons: If the Royals make it to the World Series, will you come to Kansas City and get tickets to the series?*
>
> *Sungwoo: Whoa! Royals can make it to the World series ever??? Korean work ethic/work circumstance is so notorious… not much vacation Usually Korean has week-long vacation in hot summer season… So I'm not sure I can get a vacation on October (So sad) But If, big If, Royals go to world series, I would try this that one?*

The Korean work ethic he speaks of is a very real thing. Following the Korean War in the late 1950s, South Koreans had to rebuild their economy with little more than guile and hard work. The website justlanded.com says of the Korean workday that "Korea has one of the highest average work weeks and overtime hours in the world. With their rigorous work ethic, you can expect to go beyond your own standards to keep up. However, if you can be committed, the people around you will, in return, be committed to you."

Sungwoo is the epitome of that work ethic — working 60 and 70 hours a week and still spending time following his Royals. This makes it all the more amazing that Sungwoo watches games now via MLB.com in the early overnight hours — often at 3AM for day games and lunch time for night games in South Korea. And he's actively watching and tweeting the entire time as well (if we can keep this a little bit of a secret from his boss that would be great).

Another voice that was key to getting Sungwoo to Kansas City was a young talk show host who, himself, was learning about the Royals. Danny Parkins is a Chicago native with an education from Syracuse. He took over the afternoon drive show at KCSP 610 Sports Radio back in 2012. The wars between the two sports talk stations here in town is an entire book in and of itself. But since he took over, Danny had managed to work his second place talk show into... a second place talk show – but he was always looking to chip away at the massive ratings lead from his competition.

His competition was the stalwart Kevin Kietzman at WHB Sports Radio 810, who has ruled the afternoon sports airwaves for over 15 years, never coming close to being toppled. (Until 2014 and the Royals pennant run.)

Knowing that, Danny was always looking for clever and unique ways to move the ratings.

When, when Parkins saw Sungwoo on Twitter and heard about his story, he also began to needle him to come to Kansas City. Parkins had Royals pitcher Danny Duffy on in 2013 and their talk turned to Twitter and the beacon of positivity that was Lee Sungwoo.

Duffy said that he was taken aback by how positive Lee was — a trait that Duffy has as well, if you've ever seen him talk. Duffy's career is a lesson in positivity, overcoming doubts and leaving baseball and injuries. He would later pitch in the 2014 postseason with an injured rib cage.

"You can't take it with you, I want to fly him here and eat BBQ with him," Duffy told Parkins on his show.

Parkins then said that he'd pitch in Royals tickets for Sungwoo if he made it to the States.

==============

On June 24, 2014, five friends got an email from Korea that would forever change our lives. It had the subject line:

F I N A L L Y... I will go to KC ;-)

Simple, yet it said it all. A 20-year bucket list item for Lee Sungwoo would be accomplished on August 4, 2014, with a 20-hour flight across 11 time zones.

The trip coincided with a bit of luck and pain. Sungwoo had decided to leave his company of 12 years and get a new job. At the same time, he decided to take an extended break and help care for his ailing father, who was suffering from complications related to lung cancer. In the middle, he was going to do something very rare in the South Korean culture. He was going to take some "me time."

> Frankly this trip to KC is big decision for me, I decide to quit my current job/company by this month.
>
> As I said several times, it's matter of getting enough time, enough off work from company.. not matter of money.
>
> There is no better time for me to get fresh with enough time and visit KC!!!
>
> This trip would be my once-in-a-life-time-dream-come-true
>
> So my wife keep saying it's not polite, not right, not the best for me to refuse friends good will offering like you suggested.
>
> Staying with you, hanging around with you, many fans & making precious memories is important because they remain with me & you for a long time.

His email was humble, asking for nothing special and that he simply wanted to go to some Royals games.

Whoops.

=============

The Sungwoo welcoming committee had just over a month to plan for his arrival on August 4. So, naturally, we procrastinated for three weeks and started planning around August 1st. We were tasked with making sure he had a place to stay. That was the responsibility of Jeff

Huerter, a broadcast technician for a local cable company. Sungwoo could crash in their guest bedroom in Lenexa, KS.

A rough agenda began to take shape, outlining the absolute "must do's" when visiting Kansas City. Frankly, this was just a listing of BBQ restaurants. There were like 12 of them. That's really the only thing you HAVE to do when visiting KC. And then there was some discussion about making sure he had a ride to the game.

The entire "plan" was just a series of emails between Huerter; Kevin Robinson, a Kansas Citian who spent time in Korea; Ethan Bryan, an author from Springfield; Dave Darby, another Royals fan from the Twitterverse; and myself. We had all only met through emails and Twitter — many of us only met IRL (in real life) at the airport when we picked him up.

Much like my trip to California with my best friends, we all had our roles and mine was to be the obnoxious one. (We call it "marketing.") That seemed like the perfect lazy task for me because I'd let Twitter do all of the heavy lifting.

On August 2, I created the hashtag #SungWooToKC and posted an article on PineTarPress.com — a leading Royals blog I write for occasionally. Within hours, it was the most read post in the site's history. The news was greeted extremely warmly by the Royals community and within a day, the news was out — Sungwoo was coming to Kansas City.

The best Royals fan to have never seen a game in person is coming to The K.

If you've spent any time around Royals fans on Twitter, you no doubt have seen or interacted with Sung Woo Lee @KoreanFan_KC. Sung Woo has been a Royals fan since the 90's and adopted the team due, in part, to the successes of the teams filled with superstars like George Brett and Frank White.

He follows every game religiously (in the middle of the night) via MLB.tv and Twitter. His eternal optimism, positive attitude and fresh perspective has been refreshing as

*many of us KC-based Royals fans sometimes struggle to
find a silver lining in being Royals fans.*

After a time in the email conversation, someone asked a critical question: "Do we know if he even speaks English?" None of us
knew. We'd only communicated by email. "Does he have any dietary
restrictions? Or need anything while he's in town?" Again. Nothing.
We knew him closely and warmly through Twitter, but hadn't really
spoken live with him. There was even the suggestion that he could
be catfishing us and turn out to be a British woman. We didn't know,
but we began to prepare for whatever.

The Royals weren't really keeping up their end of the bargain in
late July either, as they were still hovering just below the .500 mark
and looking flat in third place as Sungwoo announced his travel
plans.

Darby and I both took the next week off of work. The Royals were
out of town until the 7th, so we planned a few events before their return. But the agenda was still very thin. We only had one time sensi-
tive piece of data to go off of — Sungwoo's time of arrival at Kansas
City International Airport — August 5, 5:40. So a few of us planned
to pick up our weary traveler at the airport and head to a nearby
sports bar to watch the Royals game. Very low key. So we thought.

TUESDAY 8/5 AGENDA

5:40 a.m. - Sungwoo Arrives - Terminal C, KCI

7 a.m. - Arrival Dinner - All Star Pizza (64th Street)

Royals @ Arizona (Win 12-2)

10 a.m. - Crash

Early on in the trip, within the first hour, really, was when it was
evident that this would be no normal trip for a normal tourist. A quiet gathering of two or three of us ended up with about 30 fans and
followers of Sungwoo's, as well as three news crews and a couple of
radio stations. It seems the media took note of #SungWooToKC as
well.

He stepped off the plane and was greeted with lights from news cameras. He realized he had taken off his Royals jersey on the short commuter plane from San Francisco to KC, which he quickly put back on. His first act of media savviness.

Seconds later he was fielding an impromptu press conference after flying 20 hours and 6,500 miles. He did an excellent job. His English was damn good.

Following Sungwoo's arrival at the airport, we caravanned to the small sports and pizza bar about a mile from the airport.

Sungwoo had very few requests of us, but the big one was that he wanted to watch a game in typical American fashion. With the Royals playing in Arizona, that meant we needed to do it from a sports bar.

Once word got out on Twitter, the small welcoming party at the bar of about seven people grew to ten, then 15, then 25. A representative of Anheuser-Busch presented Sungwoo with a "gift bag" of jerseys and shirts and a Chiefs hat. Several others all greeted him warmly with a hug or a handshake, and we started to settle into our chairs for a "normal" game on the televisions.

The apple pie and a new friend

Normal until the man with the apple pie walked in. "I heard about this on the radio and I thought you should have something American. So I swung by the grocery store and brought you an apple pie." Sungwoo, still jet lagged from his 20-hour journey and possibly feeling the effects of the Bud Light and Boulevard beer that was set in front of him, bowed gently and said, "Thank you." He posed for a picture with the man and the apple pie and then went back to quietly watching the Royals game in the pizza bar.

This was the surreal moment when we realized this wasn't an ordinary guy. This wasn't even an extraordinary guy. This was a special guy and people were trying to find some way to reflect how special the whole thing was.

Midwestern hospitality is hard to describe. On the surface, it's little more than maybe a smile walking past someone, but there are deeper levels. In many ways it must be earned, but once it has been, the door is completely open and the generosity is overpowering. The evidence for Sungwoo to win the heart of the heartland was the years of losing that he had endured watching the Royals from 6,500 miles away.

But in all other respects, he is a Kansas Citian. This was a homecoming and no homecoming is complete without apple pie.

Chapter 6

The Seoul of Baseball

Lee Sungwoo and Negro Leagues Museum President Bob Kendrick talking about Jackie Robinson

Kansas City is split into five major areas — Overland Park on the Kansas side, Downtown KC on the Missouri side. Independence and parts south on the east side of town, and then Olathe south of Overland Park. The Northland is anything north of the Missouri River and is the part of town I grew up in. I have lived in Kansas City for all but two of my 42 years.

There are no major landmarks or tourist attractions in the Northland except for maybe the theme park, Worlds of Fun. The more famous sites are reserved mostly for downtown, Overland Park, and the east side of town where Kauffman and Arrowhead stadiums are. So as a Northland guy, we were never terribly close to Kansas City's attractions and her history.

So I relied on my new friends in the welcoming committee to suggest great things to do (other than eat all of the BBQ in town) while Sungwoo was in the city. As a baseball fan, however, the absolute first thing anyone needs to do on a first day in town is drive directly to the Negro Leagues Baseball Museum in the historic 18th and Vine District made famous by the old Blues tune "Kansas City."

WEDNESDAY 8/6 AGENDA

10 a.m. - Negro Leagues Museum

11:30 a.m. - Lunch @ Bryant's BBQ

Noon - WWI Museum/Liberty Memorial

4 p.m. - Boulevard Brewery Tour

Royals @ Arizona (Win 4-2)

The wonderful museum has been the subject of dozens of incredible articles and books, most notably the book *The Soul of Baseball* by Joe Posnanski. It is a magical place filled with the history of our nation and how baseball wove its way through those events. It was our first stop and one of the most emotional.

Sungwoo was well aware of the story of the Negro leagues and Jackie Robinson, but it hits you in a completely different way when you walk through the doors to the Negro Leagues Museum.

The ghost of the great John "Buck" O'Neil greets you as you walk in the door, and he is ever present in the museum he helped build and in every stitch of the story he helped knit. On day one, Sungwoo was now standing in one of the holiest Meccas in the religion of Baseball.

Touring him around is the NLBM President Bob Kendrick, who spends 90 minutes telling him about the most terrible and wonderful period of American history — the segregation and the desegregation of American baseball. Kansas City is home to the greatest Negro Leagues team of all time, the Kansas City Monarchs, who only had one losing season. Lee turned to Kendrick and cocked his head as he coyly said, "Mr. Kendrick, the Monarchs only had one losing season? Who is THEIR General Manager?" The line drew a sly grin on the faces of some of those standing around the conversation, those who knew that the Royals' General Manager made no moves at the baseball trade deadline the week before — much to the chagrin of Sungwoo and other Royals fans.

As we planned this, we still had no idea if Sungwoo spoke conversational English, so we were preparing ourselves for the possibility that he did not. Once we realized he spoke better English than me after a couple of drinks, we rescinded our request for translators, but since this was the first event, we had already lined up a couple of students from a local prep academy to help out. The event was as emotional for them as anyone on the trip. In talking with their sponsor who also came with us, he said it would be the most educational thing they did all year.

As we arrived, there was a stir amongst those already at the museum. There were about seven of us total, but as we completed our tour an hour later, the group had swelled to 30 or 40 — on a random Wednesday in August. Sungwoo, as he would do throughout the entire trip, took every "selka" (selfie) picture, and shook every hand with those who decided to join us on the impromptu trip to the Negro Leagues Museum. Two more news crews showed up as well. This was turning into a thing.

Sungwoo, meet the great John "Buck" O'Neill

Day one continued with lunch at Bryant's BBQ down the street, my personal favorite BBQ place in town, and I was proud it was the first KC BBQ he had. (As Kansas City Mayor Sly James frequently says, though, choosing your favorite KC BBQ joint is like picking which of your children is your favorite. You might have one, but you're wise to never say it out loud.)

What was planned for about five of us for lunch swelled to nearly 20 people chomping down on the tangy goodness of my favorite BBQ in my favorite town. Sungwoo hadn't eaten anything quite like Bryant's, yet that didn't stop him from digging into the burnt ends and ribs in what would later cause an international gastrointestinal incident.

We were already seeing the agenda move and shift, and that meant Sungwoo having to do his first radio interview with 610 Sports Radio's Danny Parkins over the phone, which radio stations generally don't like to do. So there we are, out in the parking lot of Bryants, with ambulances driving by and Sungwoo still trying to get his head around his first tastes of KC BBQ.

If that was just the story, this whole thing goes away, but something happened on that first day Sungwoo was in Kansas City — he won us over. He attacked this town with this effervescent charm. His knowledge of the Royals was incredible as well.

The interview lasted about ten minutes and at this point, his English was still plodding and deliberate.

He retold the story of how he started to follow baseball and then the Royals and the Jeff King homer. He was engaging and funny and warm and soft spoken. But the next question endeared him to the most diehard Royals fans and that was the money shot.

Parkins asked Sungwoo who his favorite Royal was. "Oh. I love all the Royals. It is not for me to choose." Parkins insisted and asked again who his favorite Royal was. "Well, I guess I love all Royals except for Neifi Perez."

To the uninitiated, you probably let this answer pass and move on to the next story. But for Royals fans who have been knee-deep in the culture of the past 29 years of losing, Neifi Perez is a tent pole around which Royals bloggers and reporters and fans draw fuel for their misery and cynicism.

Perez was famously traded for fan favorite Jermaine Dye in 2001. Perez was a highly touted, slick-fielding shortstop with next to no offensive prowess. In reality, he was a $4 million dollar bucket of dead weight on the team. He once refused to go into a game, and his career ended surrounding drug-use rumors. He is widely considered one of the worst players to ever put on a Royals uniform, and Sungwoo's reference instantly earned him street cred with the fanbase.

Sungwoo was winning over Kansas City at a time that this city needed something to cheer for.

Chapter 7
The K

(from left to right) My cousin Ron, my sister Cathy (kneeling) and myself (in bear hat) at the 1985 World Series parade at Crown Center, Kansas City, MO)

Thousands of us have grown up at Kauffman Stadium. My cousin Ronnie and I were no exception. The Royals began in 1969, we were born in 1972, and we began frequenting The K (then called Royals Stadium) shortly thereafter.

At first, we'd go with my dad who got tickets from his employer, Kansas City Power & Light, where he worked for 30 years as their head chemist. We'd sit in the lower level behind the first base dugout about 30 rows up. Today, those are considered prime seats, and through the eyes of a five or six year old, the stadium looked enormous.

Ever the introvert, The K became my stage. I would sing "Take Me Out to the Ball Game" intentionally off key. One time a man gave me a dollar to go sit somewhere else, much to the amusement of my father, who appreciated the distance as he had to drive me home as well where I gave a repeat performance.

I was a fan of "Big" John Mayberry and Freddie Patek, almost the largest and smallest Royals to ever play on the same diamond. "BIG JOHN!" I would scream when his name was called — again, much to the chagrin of those sitting around us. I quickly learned that if you wanted to be loud in life, a baseball stadium was a great place to do it.

Royals Stadium became my stomping grounds with Ronnie as we would frequently be dropped off at the top of Blue Ridge Cutoff outside the stadium (back when you were allowed to do such things) and we'd just find a way in. My cousin was a grafter-in-waiting and we'd either talk our way into the park or walk through the central tunnel the vendors would walk in. We'd go early for batting practice. We'd collect dozens of baseballs. We'd watch so much baseball that we could tell you the entire 25-man roster from Willie Aikens to Joe Zdeb.

I knew every nook and cranny both before and after the renovation as the name evolved into Kauffman Stadium.

So in 2014, I was extremely excited to introduce Sungwoo to *my* baseball stadium.

THURSDAY 8/7 AGENDA

8:45 a.m. - Radio Interviews at 610 Sports, 980 NewsRadio and 96.5 The Buzz

2 p.m. - Kauffman Stadium Tour

5:30 p.m. - Arrowhead Stadium Tour

7 p.m. - Chiefs vs. Bengals Chiefs Won 41-39

Royals @ Arizona (Win 6-2)

The day Sungwoo arrived, we still had no formal plans to tour the park and the team was out of town for the next few days. Our best guess was that we'd just drive there on the off day and ask to walk around. Once the media attention began on that Wednesday, I got a call soon after from someone with the Royals asking if we were doing anything that day. Well, we really didn't have any plans other than attacking Sungwoo's digestive system with more burnt ends and baked beans. So we showed up at 11 not knowing what was in store.

We were met by several members of the front office of the Royals down in the lobby of Kauffman Stadium and a television crew. "Sungwoo, we are very excited to introduce you to Kauffman Stadium," Toby Cook, the Vice President for the Royals, told him. He continued to shake his head like he didn't believe this moment was really happening.

Also walking along with us was a quiet young woman carrying a couple of Royals items. Her name was Jennifer Splittorff, the daughter of Royals Hall of Fame pitcher Paul Splittorff. Splitt was one of the all-time Royals greats not only as a left-handed pitcher, but also as a team broadcaster for over a decade.

Jennifer's father passed away several years ago, but she showed up at Kauffman Stadium carrying a "Little Splitty" Bobblehead and a patch the team wore the year after Splittorff passed away embroidered with SPLITT. She wasn't asked by the Royals to attend, but with tears in HER eyes, she leaned over and told me, "For some reason I just felt I needed to be here."

I remember my cousin Ronnie and I running up and down the spirals and all over every nook and cranny of the stadium. We were a security guard's worst nightmare. Yet as we began the tour, we started in areas I'd never seen before even with a press pass. We visited the opposing team's clubhouse, the batting cages behind the dugout and the press box.

The Royals presented a personalized 23 "SUNGWOO" jersey from Royals greeter "KayCee" (Dave Webster), ambassador of the Royals Hall of Fame, and we walked underneath the mammoth Crown Vision video board. He picked the 23 for Zack Greinke, Sungwoo's favorite all-time Royal. Twenty-three was also the number of current Royal Nori Aoki and former Royals Mark Gubicza and Sungwoo's Twitter friend Danny Duffy. But it was Duffy that Sungwoo saw with 23.

It was almost like he was being recruited to play football at Notre Dame. The guy had free reign of the place.

In the visitor's clubhouse, we lounged on the couches as if we had just played a double-header, and we dreamt of the unlimited amount of bubble gum and sunflower seeds that were the spoils of Major League ballplayers. We took the elevator to the upper level of Kauffman Stadium — the 400 level seats — and Sungwoo insisted on climbing the steps all the way up to the top to take a picture of Kauffman in all her glory. He was reliving memories from my youth, as no trip was complete for Ronnie and me before we did the exact same thing.

Those of us who live and attend games here frequently are often concerned at how Kauffman Stadium looks to outsiders. Kansas City is notoriously defensive about our standing in the world even as progress continues here in town. Kansas City was named one of the best cities in America by *The Huffington Post* recently, which led to a long conversation about all of its failings. The city hosted the 2012 All-Star game flawlessly and would go on to host the 2014 World Series, yet folks around here kept pointing out the pimples as the rest of the beauty glowed.

At the All-Star Game, fans were nervous about how The K would look on television. It has kind of a noisy backdrop with a Denny's and a vocational college in the background, not to mention the busy Interstate 70 just beyond left field. But you'd never have any concerns if you saw Sungwoo's face. Kauffman looked just fine. The ear-to-ear smile confirmed it.

During the tour of the Royals Hall of Fame, Sungwoo stopped at a photo of a lanky left-hander, pasty-skinned pitcher clearly from the early days of the Royals history. He began mimicking the positioning of the awkward-looking pitcher. Jennifer Splittorff came up behind him and said, "that's my dad." Sure enough, in the small print next to the picture was a description of some of the awkward warmups pitchers would go through in spring training. At that point, she knew she had made the right decision. Her dad would've loved to introduce Sungwoo to his stadium.

But it was the offer to step on the field that was the ultimate magical moment. Twenty years. Twenty years and an insistence by his wife and ailing father had come down to this. Twenty years and a fluke Jeff King homer — and he was about to touch the field that he'd dreamt of for so long. The group of now 20 that started with a handful of friends and then included several stadium workers and front office personnel that all wanted to see the traveler from South Korea began to allow him his space. This was his moment. All alone.

He stepped up the dugout steps and gestured for us to join him. No. This, he needed to do on his own.

The great comedian Billy Crystal has always talked about thinking Yankees Stadium was a cathedral as a child. A location that was Holy. Special. Poets and authors have spilled ink barrels talking about the first time they laid their eyes on a ballpark in their youth. It was something that Crystal and Ronnie and myself and thousands of us all grew up experiencing.

But this was different. This was a 38-year-old man who had only seen Kauffman Stadium from a television or computer screen. He had never smelled the grass. The pine tar. The dirt. He never felt the gravel underneath his shoes or squinted up into the sun imagining a pop fly heading his way.

Until today.

He kneeled and he touched the grass and he wept.

Thousands of miles and two decades to touch the grass at Kauffman Stadium

Chapter 8

The Perfect Day

The Perfect Night - Cousin Ron, his son Jack, my son Brett and myself.
(Originally written in July, 2007)

We were so excited to see the fireworks.

Every Friday, the Royals shoot fireworks off after their games. I had finally, after many years, convinced my four-year-old, Brett, to like fireworks. This would be my first opportunity to take him to a fireworks show that he was actually looking forward to without deteriorating into a mass of tears.

Accompanying me would be my cousin Ronnie and his five-year-old boy, Jack. Due to a recent car accident, Ronnie would be confined to a wheelchair, but was very eager to get out of the house and enjoy a ballgame with his old friend.

Like a Swiss watchmaker, I had it delicately planned out; it would be the perfect day. I would pick up Ronnie and Jack so that we'd arrive in the second inning or so, that way, it would cut down the waiting time for the boys between arrival and fireworks. You see, when you have four- and five-year-olds out, there is an unspoken clock that goes off after 9:00 p.m. And fireworks weren't supposed to start until about 9:30 or so. So, being proactive was key. But it's just like most events we go to, right? What could be different about this one?

Picking up Ronnie gave me the opportunity, no... the *privilege* to drive his special wheelchair van. The van had all the comfort that you hear about on those Cadillac commercials with the guy from Fantasy Island... "the rich... Corinthian leather..." the struts and shocks from the Nixon administration... the rack-and-pinion steering... the handle to open the front door, just like a school bus... yes, this thing had it ALL! And I was driving it.

Now, I haven't spent a lot of time with my cousin since his accident. And I think he was shy to tell me if he needed anything. But his chair answered the questions for me. Every bump in the road that I hit with the bus, his chair let out a huge "BEEEEEEP." Now, if any of you have driven in Missouri, you know that you can't swing a dead cat and not hit a bump. Needless to say, it was a beepy ride.

But still... fireworks awaited.

On the way to the game, Jack and Brett talked about what most four and five year olds talk about – which is technically just one level above babble. Topics ranged from whose mommy snored louder (my wife won that one hands down) to the never stale topic of farts.

Jack even had a short power-nap. Hmmm... a power-nap at 7:00? Must just be tired.

But we soon saw the stadium lights over the horizon and knew our wait was just about over. Pulling into the parking lot and driving the babe-magnet short-bus, I knew I'd have the rare privilege of parking in the front row handicapped space.

Um, that was, if they weren't all full.

Remember before, when I said we'd arrive late to be smarter than Swiss watch maker or some such? Yeah, it also meant driving to four different lots trying to find a parking spot with that little wheelchair guy on it.

When NASA launches the space shuttle, they have that T-Minus clock. In my head, this clock read about T-Minus 120 minutes until fireworks. Well, someone had to get out the calculator and add about 20 minutes of driving around the parking lot. T-Minus 140 minutes, indeed.

Finally, I pulled up to one of those helpful stadium traffic guys with the light sabers.

"Hey, I've been driving forever, where the hell can I park this thing?"

"Um. How about right there?"

Yes, he literally let me just park right on the curb in front of the stadium. The logic was impeccable. What were they going to do, tow the short-bus? I think not. So I turned off the key and parked at the doorstep to Royals Stadium like I was delivering a pizza..

Oh… wait… in order to open the back of the ramp, you've got to turn the key on. Sorry. Forgot that part.

The game had just started, we were approaching the ballpark. We were almost in the stadium. All we had to do was pick up our tickets.

Like I said earlier, I had it all planned. I called the ticket office earlier in the day and ordered tickets in the special wheelchair section so there'd be no delay getting in the stadium. "Just go to any box office and they'll take care of you," the gleeful man on the phone told me.

By "take care of you" I think he meant, "jerk you around."

I went to "any" box office. "Any", to me, is defined as "the closest" or "the most accommodating."

To the Kansas City Royals, "any" was defined as "the main ticket office on the other side of where you parked." A cheerful, elderly, nearly dead and certainly pissed off about it woman named Esther explained that to me.

Now, I am a guy who has a healthy respect for pride. I smile at nuns when walking down the street because I respect them and I think they appreciate it. I try to do the right thing most of the time.

I would certainly never use my cousin's disability for my own personal gain. That is, until Ester told me I had to walk clear around the stadium for my tickets. My ethics, and probably most of Ronnie's pride, went right out the window.

"Esther... do you see that man behind me? The man in the wheel-chair? You're telling me that I need to go clear around to the..."

Ester interrupted... "You do if you want your tickets."

Okay. So Esther wasn't operating on the same spiritual level as I was. We packed up and headed to the "Main" box office.

But it was only the bottom of the first. We still had a very enjoy-able evening ahead of us.

Brett and I walked hand-in-hand across the parking lot. Jack was sleeping restfully in Ron's lap as he rolled behind us.

Aw... that's cute. Jack looks so peaceful. Hmmm... its 7:30, he must just be tired.

Inside the gates, we can see all the families walking to their seats. But we'll be there soon enough. Besides, nothing happens in the first innings anyway.

Just then, I heard the roar of the crowd. The faint signal of the sta-dium radio broadcast explaining that my favorite player, Billy Butler had just hit a 3-run home run in the bottom of the first.

With tickets in hand, we take the long elevator ride (it's only one floor down, but the Kauffman Stadium elevators are from World War I) to our section.

It's now the bottom of the second and we finally pull into our seats right behind home plate in the handicapped section. Jack had finally woken up. Brett and I sit down and I'm taking orders for my first run to the concession stand.

Ron wants frosty malt. Brett wants some peanuts. Jack wants some... Jack, I can't hear you. Speak up.

"...throw... up..."

What?? That kind of sounded like hot dog, right??

"...I have... to... be... sick..." Jack's face turned the same color of white as the marshmallow colored van we drove here in. Then it turned a little green.

He leaped into my arms and immediately I started on this O.J. Simpson dash towards the nearest restroom. You know the one, where O.J. starts leaping over luggage carts trying to make it to the airport gate on time? With my gazelle-like quickness, it should be no problem.

I got approximately 2 1/2 steps and barely turned around to the concourse when it happened. The kind of vomit that starts at your shoes and propels its way out in a parabolic arc that seems to stop time.

Puke, all over me. All over the sidewalk behind us and then my inner O.J. kicked in... leaving a trail of vomit behind me, all the way to the restroom.

Yep. Jack was sleeping because he wasn't feeling good. Just then I realized that my future as a doctor was up in smoke. Not Dr. Spock, not Dr. Quinn, Medicine Woman, heck, not even Dr. Phil.

Once his stomach was empty, I took Jack to the first aid room so he could lie down and get a cool cloth on his head. We'd been gone about ten minutes when I realize I've left his paralyzed father and my 4 year old boy wondering where the hell we just went. Last they know, we went for some hot dogs.

I had the nurse stay with Jack when I went and told Ronnie what happened. He went to fetch Jack as the stadium custodial crew was working on cleaning up Jack's breakfast and lunch from the side-walk.

And with all the sincerity that a four-year-old can muster, my son Brett asked, "Daddy, did you bring me back my peanuts?"

It's now the 4th inning and Ronnie has just returned from First Aid with Jack. Jack was feeling better. I know this because he just asked his Uncle Chris for cotton candy and a hot dog.

I went and headed towards the concession stand, careful to step over the yellow "BIOHAZARD" towels draped over what happened my last time I was on this sidewalk.

I bought Ron his frosty malt, got a hot dog for me, peanuts for my boy and I got Jack a Gatorade.

"Where's my hot dog?"

Um… Jack, let's wait a couple innings before we put anything on your stomach, okay?

"Daddy, I want a hot dog," Brett said with precision comic timing.

The next several minutes a pout-fest of Biblical proportions ensued when both boys turned on the charm. Ronnie broke first and he and Jack went to get him a hot dog.

Ah… I finally get to sit down and watch the game. Gosh, it's already the 6th inning.

"Hey, Chris."

I turned around to see one of my best friends from my old job, Angie. She had this wry smile on her face as she sat in the seat next to me.

"So… you're having a little bit of a day?"

I replied, "What do you mean?"

"Um… wasn't that you I just saw carrying a five-year-old like a football with puke streaming from his mouth?"

I immediately began to cover the vomit stain on my sleeve… and my collar… and my front. "Um, nope?"

"Yeah, my whole section really felt sorry for you."

Oh… my… God… Tell me no one that I actually knew saw that.

Angie stayed only about three minutes talking, but it seemed like two hours. My humiliation was building, but hey, we're here to see fireworks, right? No one is dead yet and we're making good progress in the game. The eternal optimist in me was kicking back in.

I waved bye to Angie and watched her as she sat in her seat about 20 rows above ours. As I was turning back to the field, I noticed the beautiful sky just beyond the scoreboard. It was amber, as the sun was setting. I looked at my son, Brett eating his hot dog. What could be better, right?

Wait… that's a little darker amber. More of a greenish, hue. And it's moving pretty fast. Well, I'm sure glad there wasn't any rain in the forecast.

Ronnie and Jack were back and we enjoyed a full inning of baseball. It was the 8th inning and we were just a few moments away from fireworks.

The sky turned an orange-green that would you only find in the largest of crayon boxes. This color was way beyond the 64-color box with the pencil sharpener. This color was reserved for some uber-collection of wax colors that consumers rejected as "too scary."

I turned to Ronnie and asked him what our contingency plan was if it started to rain.

"I can't get the chair wet. It's got a lot of electrical parts in it."

No sooner had he finished the sentence than the skies unleashed a rain shower that my father would have described as "a cow pissing on a flat rock."

That's okay, we're only a few feet from the service tunnel. Well, there were about 50 people between us and the service tunnel.

We finally made it through the crowd and underneath the stands. The crowds were still very thick so we made it over to where the service elevators were. There were only a couple of wheelchairs and some equipment there, so that's where we found respite from the storm.

We had to make that hard decision that everyone in the stadium was making right then. Should we stay, or should we go? The boys' mothers would have easily decided to bail and head for home, dragging saddened and crying boys away. But Ronnie and I, with the same level of insanity that Clark W. Griswold employed in *Vacation*, decided to see some God damn fireworks. We've come all this way, and we're not going back now.

We had some cover, the boys were having a good time running around each other and there's only one inning left between us and fireworks. We decided to wait it out.

When Ronnie and I were young, we were the equivalent of frick and frack. We went everywhere together. Best friends. One of our favorite haunts was Kauffman, then Royals, Stadium.

Aunt Mary would drop us off at the top of the hill above the stadium and then wave to us telling us to call when she needed to pick us up.

Ronnie and I would then go on an adventure spree seen only by escaped convicts and cockroaches. We would sneak into restricted areas of the stadium, we would run up and down the spirals, we would bring fishing nets to the games to lower them down to field-level so players would put foul balls in them. I remember going to Ronnie's house one time to find two giant buckets of Major League baseballs.

The point is, that there wasn't anything mischievous that we hadn't done in that stadium.

Well... almost anything...

Ronnie was starting to get tired. But he gestured over to the security guard and whispered in my ear.... "ask that guy to go get that fishing net he stole from me 20 years ago."

I chuckled... it was a nice moment. He's been through a lot this past year, but his humor has always been...........

VROOM... EEEERRRRRKKKKKKKKKKKKKK

Oh shit. Where were Jack and Brett?

Ronnie and I turned around to see Jack on a John Deere 4×4 Gator lurching towards a service door with Brett hanging on the back. His legs were apparently just long enough to reach the gas pedal.

Now, he only went about ten feet forward. But I'm sure as I retell this story to people, I'll have him as far as Blue Ridge Mall.

Oh shit. Oh shit. Oh shit.

They couldn't kick a guy in a wheelchair, his son and his idiot cousin and his son out of a game, could they?

Luckily, the security guard's eagle-eyes, which were powerful enough to spot Ronnie's fishing net 20 years ago, were now closed as he was taking a short nap in his chair. We were safe. The boys were in no trouble.

Ronnie and I had never stolen a four-wheeler at the stadium before. Chalk one up to the future generation.

Another security guard walked by us and said that they were pulling the tarp and getting ready to resume the game.

Figuring that we shouldn't hang around the scene of the crime any longer, we returned to our soggy seats.

Remember when I said that there is this internal clock in children and it starts to go haywire after 9:30? Well, it's now 10:05 and the children are behind us leading the entire vomit-witnessing section in "LET'S GO ROYALS" chants. They were on fire.

Some stadium workers even walked by them and gave them very special pins that said "SUPER FANS" on them.

There was only one more out to go. As fate would allow it, someone above decided that we'd had enough drama and got a three-pitch strikeout to end the game.

The lights dimmed, the boys both climbed into our respective laps and the fireworks show began.

We made it.

The fireworks show was awesome. Every week they have a theme for their music, and tonight was the music of Dean Martin. Pretty cool.

We filed out of the stadium. Ronnie glared at that security guard as we loaded the elevator to head to the parking level. We loaded up the short-bus. Ronnie's chair beeped as I started the van like some R2-D2 robot in a pissy mood.

Brett and Jack resumed their point-counterpoint debate about whose daddy snores loudest. (The Kamler family went 2 for 2 in that contest, by the way.)

Then the van went quiet. Even though the shocks were still taking a beating on the I-70 asphalt, even though Ronnie's chair was beeping like the stock market had just crashed and I even managed to stop my yapping about the vomit all over my shirt. The van just went completely… silent.

And I hear the youngest person in the van speak loudly and confidently as he said…

"You know, Daddy, this was the perfect day."

Chapter 9

The Minors & The Inflatable Ball

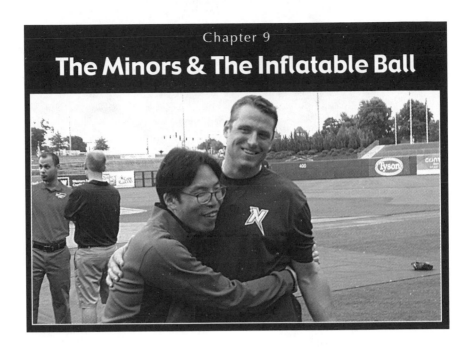

The #SungWooToKC adventure really only had a few simple goals. See the city. Meet other fans. Watch Royals games. The problem with his arrival was that the Royals were finishing up a six game West Coast road trip in Arizona, so we actually had a couple of days to kill in the city before the Boys in Blue made it back to The K.

"I want to go to a minor league," Sungwoo insisted. There are two minor league Royals affiliate farm clubs within a day trip from Kansas City. There's the Omaha Storm Chasers about three hours northwest in Nebraska, and the Northwest Arkansas Naturals about three hours southeast along the Missouri-Arkansas border in Springdale. The AAA Storm Chasers were on their own road trip, but the Naturals were at home. So on Friday, we headed south to check out the AA farm club of the Royals.

We left around noon, which didn't allow for much time in the Springdale area. There are four cities that make up "Northwest Arkansas" — Rogers, Springdale, Fayetteville and Bentonville. Fayetteville is the home of the University of Arkansas; Bentonville is the home to the corporation Wal-Mart. The entire cluster of small cities, even including the city of Joplin, Missouri about an hour

FRIDAY 8/8 AGENDA

11:00 AM	Depart for Northwest Arkansas
4:00 PM	Tour Arvest Park
7:00 PM	NWA Naturals vs. San Antonio Missions Naturals (lost 6-2), San Francisco at Royals (Win 4-2)
11:00 PM	Depart NWA for Kansas City
2:00 AM	Arrive in Kansas City

north, is an incredible area. You have some amazing nature including all that the Ozark Mountains have to offer, but then you've also got this incredible bustling city in Bentonville as companies have moved around Wal-Mart to help support their retail agreements.

Bentonville is also the home of Royals owner David Glass, who has had his ups and downs as owner of the franchise.

We were running behind and wanted to tour the ballpark before the game, so about six or seven of us arrived at Arvest Ballpark (Arvest is a local bank) around four to be met by several "tweeps" (i.e., Twitter friends) and now there were close to fifteen of us. We walked in and were greeted by Justin Cole, the General Manager of the club. (Being a general manager of a AA farm club isn't quite as glamorous as being Dayton Moore, but Sungwoo treated him with the same level of respect.) We began the tour by watching a passing rain shower go by, and then our gracious GM host joined with the rest of the front office staff in pulling off the tarp so the team could get batting practice in. (See? I told you it wasn't glamorous.)

Once the team took the field, we were invited down to watch batting practice and take some photos in the dugout. Sungwoo was over the moon. This was his first opportunity to see professional athletes up close. So close he could touch them. And then he started handing out hugs. Many of them. He met Royals prospect Hunter Dozier, an athletic kid with a ton of potential, and Sungwoo bear hugged him within an inch of his life.

The greatest hug was reserved for former Royals outfielder Mitch Maier, who had just signed a minor league contract with the Nat-

Figure 12 - The Arkansas chapter of the Welcoming Committee

urals for one last summer in the sun. When he signed the contract and was shipped to AA, we all assumed it was to groom him to be a coach, but on this day, he was taking batting practice and nursing a back injury. We're not sure the status of that back injury after Sungwoo saw him with a squeal and a "MISH-MI-IER!!! MISH-MI-IER!!!" and then proceeded to hug the living crap out of this six-year MLB veteran.

The players were friendly enough, but they had no idea who Sungwoo was and went on about their business. That's when former Mets catcher Vance Wilson, now the manager for the Naturals, was informed of the special guest. "Hey Sungwoo, come up here and watch batting practice with us."

Sungwoo got to stand on the stoop just outside the batting cage and watch future major leaguers take their cuts. Up close, there is absolutely nothing like watching the speed and the power of a truly perfect baseball swing, and the batting cage is an amazing place to watch from.

Following batting practice, the group all figured we'd just head to dinner before the game or just hang out in the light drizzle, but Wilson had other plans. "Hey Sungwoo, how about you and your friends come down to the clubhouse with us?"

It was the type of moment that Sungwoo and this lifelong baseball fan were stunned by. It was the same as Shoeless Joe Jackson asking Terrence Mann to come to the corn with the guys in *Field of Dreams*.

I've spent the last few years covering the Royals for the *Platte County* [MO] *Landmark*, which gives me a media pass about seven or eight times a year. So I know that ballplayers are very protective of their clubhouse — even the name implies the type of mentality that their treehouse would have a "NO OUTSIDERS ALLOWED" sign on the outside. So I recognized that this was big deal.

But this was Sungwoo's chance to shine. Into the clubhouse we went. As the club had just finished up BP, they were eating dinner before the game. Wilson stepped to the Knute Rockne spot in the middle of the clubhouse and cut the silence, "Hey guys, listen up. I want you all to meet this guy Sungwoo. He came a long way to meet you all."

One by one, the players put down their paper plate of chicken and pasta and came up to shake Sungwoo's hand. There was third baseman Cheslor Cuthbert, a future major leaguer if there ever was one, with bulging biceps but meekly going up and introducing himself to the foreign visitor. "You are Cheslor Cuthbert!!! Oh my gosh!!" Sungwoo was in heaven.

The life of a minor leaguer is humbling in many ways. Even if you're a bonus baby or a big deal, the anonymity of the minor leagues can really take you down a peg — especially in Northwest Arkansas, when you're constantly struggling for attention between SEC Arkansas football and baseball. These kids know they're a big deal because they are professional ballplayers, yet they don't quite have the self-confidence to strut it out. So they would slowly approach us, head bowed, and say their names. On sight and with 99% accuracy, Sungwoo would finish their sentences with the entire roster of the Naturals. He nailed them all. Ethan Chapman. Hunter Dozier. Lane Adams. Justin Trapp. He knew them all by sight. And when he met Jorge Bonifacio, he recalled "your brother used to play for the Royals." And he was right, brother Emilio Bonifacio was a platoon infielder in 2013.

Sungwoo's street cred with Royals baseball fans, players and all of us was growing exponentially. After meeting nearly the entire team, we said our goodbyes and as we were leaving, Wilson presented Sungwoo with an autographed copy of the 11x17 lineup card from the night before. An extremely generous gesture.

But before we left the private confines of the clubhouse, there was one more player who had walked by. Off the main hallway where the clubhouse is, there is a weight room, and one player was toweling off as he was finishing his workout. "Um, excuse me, you are Ed-I-son Reen-cone you play third base, yes?"

Rincone kind of stopped in his tracks and clearly wasn't aware of why this man was halting him from dinner and a baseball game with a posse of eight other strangers. He seemed a little miffed at the question, "Naw man, I play outfield."

To myself I thought, "Oh well, Sungwoo couldn't get them all right." And he said how nice it was to meet him and we walked out the clubhouse door. But Sungwoo was insistent that this man, a total stranger until seconds ago, was a third baseman. He was mumbling under his breath as we walked back out into the hallway. "That was Ed-I-son Reen-cone. He play third base." I mean, even the greatest baseball players strike out every once in a while.

That's when one of the coaches stopped us and kind of leaned in, "Yeah, he just changed positions about a month ago and he's still a little crabby about it."

Sungwoo's rock star Royals street cred was restored.

The absolute best thing about minor league baseball has nothing to do with the play on the field. In fact, it's usually pretty awful. My son and I like to take a weekend every year and visit a different minor league ballpark, and this year we went to the Royals Class A affiliate, the Legends baseball club in Lexington, Kentucky.

The baseball was the same as a good high school program or maybe a junior college program. But you learn to watch for the kids that stand out, and they do. For baseball fans, that's what you do at minor league baseball games.

But there are honestly very few pure baseball fans at a minor league game. Most are just out for fun. MiLB will do just about anything to draw crowds out to the games. That means promotions and really great food.

After our amazing trip through the private sanctuary of the Northwest Arkansas clubhouse, our heads were still spinning. The good news is that we timed it so the concession stands were just about to open.

Every minor league park has a signature food. Werner Park, where the AAA Omaha Storm Chasers play, has a really great Reuben sandwich right behind home plate. With Omaha being the birthplace of the Reuben, I make sure to get one every time I'm there. Community America, where the Kansas City T-Bones play, has a ribeye sandwich which is pretty decent. Whitaker Park in Lexington had a Donut PB&J sandwich which is a Krispy Kreme donut sliced in half, filled with peanut butter and jelly and then reassembled. It's an acquired taste.

But Arvest ballpark has something that is known throughout baseball — it is the deep fried funnel dog. It. Is. Glorious.

It's a corndog coated in funnel cake batter and then deep fried. You can get it served with powdered sugar as well. So in one bite you've got the sweet from the powdered sugar, the cake taste, and then the juicy hot dog goodness all in one orgy of taste in your mouth. Yeah. I said it. An orgy of taste in your mouth.

I happen to get it without the powdered sugar, but with the ketchup/mustard mixture that I perfected in middle school as a corndog connoisseur. There is a perfect ratio that might take another book to fully explain. But I get it every time I'm at NWA and it's amazing.

And the prices are amazingly reasonable as well. You can get the funnel dog for $3 along with a beer or a coke for less than $6.

After stuffing ourselves full of empty calories, it was time for the game. Suddenly Sungwoo was nowhere to be found. The minor league mascots were announced on the field. Riding in on the back of a pickup truck, amongst the two Naturals mascots Strike and Sinker (yes there are two), stood Sungwoo waving to everyone.

The Law Firm of Strike, Sinker, and Sungwoo (photo by Josh Boring)

Promotions at a minor league stadium are as critical to the fabric of the country as cheesesteak and apple pie. There's the dizzy bat race — where two kids have to spin around a bat until they're dizzy, then complete some sort of obstacle course. There's also some really fun games like lawn bowling, golf chip shots and giant dice. But I was unfamiliar with the inflatable ball race.

During the sixth inning, Sungwoo disappeared again only to re-appear inside of a seven foot tall inflatable gerbil wheel. The goal of the game was some sort of human bowling exercise. Despite the stupidity of the entire event, all you could see was the smile on Sungwoo's face as he charged down the left field foul line to crash into three plastic inflatable pins.

His reward for his accomplishment, and I wish I was lying about this, was a year's supply of lip balm.

Minor League Baseball is its own special brand of entertainment, and getting people out to the park is a special kind of challenge. But the Naturals do it so easily and with a tongue firmly in their cheek. They were tremendous hosts and classy while we were down there.

The final promotion of the night — which had now stretched late into the evening hours meaning our return trip to Kansas City would be well into the next day — was a "Shirts off Their Backs" promotion. The Naturals were wearing customized pink jerseys for breast cancer awareness and the promotion was that you could bid on the actual shirts. Following the game, the players would remove their game used jerseys, sign them and give them to the winning bidder.

Of course we wouldn't have time to stay for that. Of course we'd leave the game early at a decent hour and get back to Kansas City before midnight, right?

Nope. That's not how Sungwoo and The Committee roll.

So of course there was a ninth inning rally to tie it up by the Naturals. Free baseball. Extra innings. The Naturals ended up losing in 14 innings and the game ended nearly as the clock struck midnight.

It would be one of only two losses Sungwoo would see while he was in the country.

Dave Darby had purchased a "shirt off their back" for Sungwoo. So following the game, he got to go down on the field and get it autographed.

The jersey?

Mitch Maier.

A signed Mitch Meier jersery right of the back of Mitch Meier (photo by Dave Darby)

Chapter 10
The Buzz

The crush of reporters and fans meeting Sungwoo in August, 2014 at KCI Airport

It's nearly impossible to predict what type of story might go viral — especially if you're in the middle of it. I had known there was a level of interest in the story from the weekend before, when I put up the #SungWooToKC hashtag. You see it retweeted on Twitter and talked about on Facebook. But you don't really know the power of something truly viral until you see it in action. Once you do see it up close, you really can only marvel at it.

We saw a handful of television cameras on Wednesday night when we met Sungwoo at the airport and that was neat. We also had a couple of interview requests on Thursday when we went around to a number of Kansas City's famous attractions, including Bryants BBQ and the Negro Leagues Museum as well as the tour of Kauffman. We went to Springdale, Arkansas on a Friday and were even met by a writer from MLB.com and a couple of local Arkansas newspapers.

One burst of interviews we did on Thursday morning was at a cluster of radio stations owned by Entercom in Overland Park. In the span of an hour, Sungwoo was on with Bob Fescoe on 610 Sports as well as Danny Parkins. He stepped down the hall to do the 980

AM news program, and then he sat in with the alternative music station here in town, 96.5 The Buzz. The morning hosts were Afentra and Danny Boi and in the 15 minute interview, they managed to get Sungwoo to spell the word W-H-O-R-E, ask him what type of beer he liked and offer to set him up with some easy girls while he was in town. It was an... interesting interview. But throughout all of it, he kept the spirit of the event. And he showed a wonderful sense of humor.

Kansas City was genuinely excited that a Royals fan traveled halfway across the globe to visit our town and bring with him such a genuine attitude. Even the folks at The Buzz walked away impressed, and their producer Mark gave Sungwoo a signed Billy Butler helmet from his personal collection.

This was all pretty interesting to see how the story evolved and was picked up in a couple places, but by no means was it more than an interesting local story before we left for Arkansas.

There is no formula for what goes "viral." One of the most famous people on YouTube is a guy named PewDiePie who has over 34 MILLION followers. Does he solve crimes? Nope. Is he a musician? No. He makes videos of himself playing video games. That's it. 34 million subscribers. I've got a friend NAJ who makes six second videos on Vine and he has amassed over 100 thousand followers six seconds at a time. Granted, his videos are hilarious.

But there's still no formula for it. I have a YouTube channel that has 15 followers. I have put up Vines and they barely are seen in the three digits. But my Twitter account has 12,000 followers. There's not much of a rhyme or reason.

I think #SungWooToKC went viral for a multitude of reasons, but they all begin and end with Sungwoo's heart and his love of the game of baseball — something this town shares with him. "He loves the stuff most people don't think about," Dave Darby told me. "He kept talking about stuff like the sound the cleats made in the dirt."

Once we got back to Kansas City on Saturday, Sungwoo was "it." People got a chance to see what he was about and know that he was real. I honestly think that is where entertainment is heading. Reality shows aren't even reality. I think people want to know people are being genuine, and there was no more "real deal" than Lee Sungwoo stepping off the plane at KCI with a look of wonderment as he glided through interviews and selfies and handshakes.

According to the tiny agenda the committee had put together, Saturday had nothing planned other than Sungwoo's first ever live Royals game. But that quickly evolved into impromptu interviews with a couple of television stations at a "small" tailgate that grew into a monster party.

SUNDAY 8/10 AGENDA

11 a.m. - Return kegs to Boulevard (all were empty)
NPR Interview at Boulevard offices

12:30 p.m. - Appearance on "Royals Live Pregame"

1 p.m. - Royals vs. Giants (Win 7-4)

5:30 p.m. - Dinner at Tengo Sed in Power & Light

6:30 p.m. - Sporting KC Watch Party
Sporting at Vancouver (Loss 2-0)

10 p.m. - Free night at Hilton President Hotel

The tailgate was an especially good example of how viral this thing had become by just day four. All I did was tweet "Tailgate. Saturday. Bring stuff." There must've been 100 people including members of the media who all brought chips, dips, cookies, dishes of BBQ, cole slaw. Whatever. Our great and wonderful friend Elizabeth Belden even brought six kegs of Boulevard beer. That significantly improved the festivities.

A fella who writes a food blog for *The Kansas City Star*, Tyler Fox, created something called "The Sungwoo Dog," which included kimchi, a Korean vegetable, burnt ends, bacon, a quail egg (pickled daikon), and other stuff. It was maybe one of best things I've ever eaten in my life.

The food was rockin', the beer was flowin' and a bottle of Korean vodka was being passed around so there's about 45 minutes of my life in the middle that were erased.

The Sungwoo Dog

There may even be video of Sungwoo and several of us shotgun-
ning a beer. This cannot be confirmed at time of press.

Sunday and Monday were a blur, with the bulk of Sungwoo's media coming during that weekend. All told, he ended up with stories
about him on ABC *World News Tonight*, the BBC, NPR's *All Things
Considered*, *The New York Times*, MLB.com, KTLA in Los Angeles and
several Korean media outlets.

On Twitter, stories and tweets of mine were being retweeted by
news outlets across the globe. We jokingly considered putting up a
Sungwoo Channel on YouTube and just letting the cameras roll for
the "Long Lost Kansas City Kardashian Sister."

This had turned into not only a thing, but THE thing as the Royals
entered the dog days of summer with every intention of wilting on
the vine, just like the 29 years previous. And suddenly I was thrust
into the role of press information director.

We got to as many requests as we could without actually cutting
into baseball watching time, and that weekend we managed to see
two Royals games, host a public tailgate for people to meet Sungwoo
(where about 150 people showed up and all of the Boulevard kegs
were consumed), made an appearance on the Fox Sports Kansas City

pregame show and received enough offers for tickets and tours and meals to set up the rest of the trip. There wasn't an event Sungwoo couldn't have attended that week.

Over the rest of the visit, Sungwoo managed to be toured around Arrowhead Stadium personally by a member of the front office. He ate at one of the fanciest restaurants in town (Grunauer), received a proclamation by the Jackson County legislature (handed to him by none other than Royals Hall of Fame second baseman Frank White), got a tour of City Hall from Mayor Sly James and met Hall of Famer George Brett, all inside a 72-hour period.

For anybody else, it might've been too overwhelming or felt like capitalizing too much on a shooting star. But it didn't feel like that at all for Sungwoo. That's the thing about the entire week. He was so gracious and genuinely humbled by the whole thing. And the outpouring of love and kindness from the folks of Kansas City and the Midwest was staggering.

Back in South Korea, SungJin followed his older brother's travels closely via social media. Sungwoo was feeling guilty for all of his adventures while his brother was staying home with his wife tending to their father who was hospitalized after suffering from pnemonia and lung cancer.

There was a bit of a backlash that Sungwoo admitted to me was occurring back home in Korea. One night we got a chance to stay in a swanky hotel downtown. So we basically had a pajama party staying up watching TV, eating garbage and reading Twitter. He showed me that his story was trending nationally back home.

Then he translated some of the not-so-nice tweets he was getting, calling him a sellout and misrepresenting that he was being paid to visit the city by the Royals (he wasn't). I asked him if that hurt his feelings at all. "I learned a new phrase while I am here in Kansas City. Haters gunna hate."

He learned a lot more stuff from us, too. Most of them aren't proper to repeat in print, but he ate it up. Any negativity didn't seem to faze him at all. He was a kid in a candy store and loving every minute of it. But he especially loved the interactions with fans.

"Hey! You're that guy!" "Hey! Welcome to Kansas City!" If we heard it once, we heard it a thousand times that week. This story doesn't happen in New York or Los Angeles or even Chicago or St. Louis simply because of the people. Kansas Citians know their lane in the world, but are extremely proud of their town. When someone chooses to come to their city or visit their attractions over the worn out and tired standards — the love shows no bounds. The entire ten-day trip was one gigantic Midwestern hug around this man from South Korea, and he returned it with every smile and selfie and event.

Chapter 11

The Memorial

Lee Sungwoo and Andrew Youngwoth at the Korean War Veterans Memorial in Leawood, KS

Andrew Youngworth is the cross country coach and Athletic Director at Carthage High School in southern Missouri. He is in his fifties and has some gray hair and the look of a distance runner. He just looks like a high school coach.

He introduced himself to us when we were in Springdale visiting the Northwest Arkansas Naturals. He asked for my phone number so that, in case he was in Kansas City later in the week, he could catch up with the Magical Mystery Tour that was the Sungwoo and his band of merry men and women. I obliged and went on with my day.

Several days later, our morning started with a radio hit at Sports Radio WHB. We were on the morning "Border Patrol" radio program, which is more disorganized chaos at times than a cohesive radio program. The show normally features four voices, and on Sungwoo day, they brought in every former Royal they could find. Jeff Montgomery and Brian McRae were both co-owners of the station, as well as former pitchers Mike Boddicker and Jaime Bluma. It was nuts.

We were heading back north when my phone rang. It was Mr. Youngworth. "I'm so glad I caught you. Can you meet me at 119th and Lowell today? I'm only in town for a few hours." We happened to be three blocks from that location and he was as well. We added a detour to the itinerary and met him at the Korean War Veterans Memorial.

119th is an extremely busy road where tens of thousands of cars travel on a given day. Although a Northlander, I had probably personally driven by the memorial a hundred times without a care.

Sungwoo and I stepped out of the car and he became immediately emotional. There was the American flag, the POW-MIA flag and the flag of South Korea waving in the breeze, alongside statues of pancho-garbed soldiers. There were tan rocks against a memorial wall built to represent the terrain of the 39th Parallel, and there was Mr. Youngworth standing with tears in his eyes.

Andy's dad Tom had had a series of health challenges over the past few months and was recovering from sepsis at a local hospital. Andy had been trekking back and forth between Carthage and Kansas City the past few weeks when he heard about Sungwoo on the radio.

After a month of surgeries in July, Andy's father was in and out of it for a while, but he heard about Sungwoo from his son. Youngworth continued, "He said, 'you need to go show him the memorial. You need to go meet him.' My dad wanted you to see this place, so I wanted to meet you here."

Tom Youngworth did not serve in Korea but was in the Armed Services during the time of the Korean War and knew Sungwoo would like to see this little slice of the 38th Parallel sitting at 119th and Lowell. Sungwoo nodded and you could tell he was thinking back to his own father, currently in a hospital in Seoul.

Sungwoo and Andy walked for 20 minutes around the small memorial, looking at the names of Kansans who fought in the war engraved in the marble. They took photographs and talked in a somber tone. I kept my distance. This wasn't my memory. This was too special.

Sungwoo handed me his camera and asked me to take a picture of him and Andy in front of the memorial. "I want to remember you and your father. I will tell my dad that we were here." Two middle-aged men both standing in front of a memorial honoring their fathers — half a world away.

Chapter 12
The Pitch & The Hall of Fame

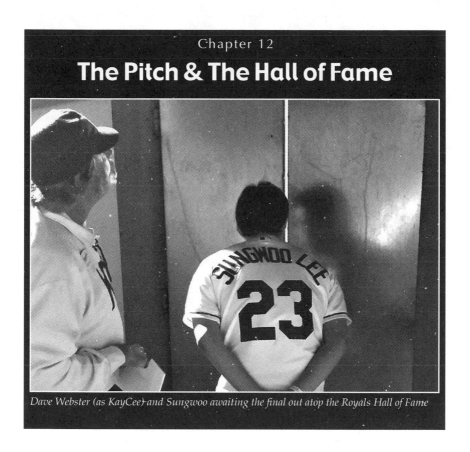

Dave Webster (as KayCee) and Sungwoo awaiting the final out atop the Royals Hall of Fame

By the middle of the trip, Sungwoo Welcoming Committee member Dave Darby and I had an unspoken rhythm. When we walked around the park with Sungwoo, one of us would take lead, then Sungwoo would walk and then the other of us — both with hulking 300-plus pound frames — would pick up the rear. This became an impromptu football wedge to the dozens of folks who would stop us for a photo or to shake his hand. Our goal wasn't to evade his fans or those that wanted to get Sungwoo to sign something or take a picture — but there were just so many that making it ten feet was nearly impossible.

He denied a total of zero handshakes. He took every photo and insisted in having as many people in pictures as possible. Often he would hand me his camera to capture the same photos as well. "For my memory. Please." And we'd walk a few more feet only to be stopped again.

A funny thing happened when Sungwoo touched down in Kansas City — the Royals started to win.

The Royals had already had a ten-game winning streak that ended on June 17th. At that time, they were 1/2 game ahead of the Detroit Tigers, or first place in the AL Central. Since that point, however, they had displayed the predictable and timely fade that Royals fans had come to expect.

The Royals had two separate four-game losing streaks in July, and bloggers and reporters began to call for Ned Yost's job as the manager of a team that couldn't hold a lead after the All-Star Break.

It was now Monday, August 11, and the day began with the most jam-packed agenda to date.

MONDAY 8/11 AGENDA

9 a.m. - Sports Radio 810

11 a.m. - Korean Memorial

Noon - Lunch

2 p.m. - Jackson County Proclamation

3:30 p.m. - Truman Presidential Library

5 p.m. - Guest for Batting Practice

6:30 p.m. - Sungwoo Throws Out First Pitch

7 p.m. - Royals vs. Oakland (Win 3-2)

We were behind schedule from the start, as the radio event lasted the entire hour and then ended with former pitcher and current pitching instructor Jaime Bluma giving Sungwoo an impromptu pitching lesson prior to his first pitch later that night. Sungwoo was terrified that he would bring dishonor to himself and the Royals by throwing out a poor first pitch. Furthermore, he was nervous that the winning streak would come to an end if he had a poor showing.

While the visit to the Korean War Memorial was extremely moving and touching, my inner project manager was nervous about getting Sungwoo all the way from the southern part of the Kansas City Metro area all the way out to Independence, where the Jackson County Legislature was holding its open session, by 2:00.

The Jackson County event almost never happened. I got a call earlier in the weekend from Lisa Carter, the press officer for the legislature, asking if Jackson County could invite Sungwoo to meet the members. Jackson County is the home county to the Kansas City Royals and Chiefs and also one of the most political institutions in the Midwest. There were PLENTY of politicians that would love a photo-op with Sungwoo, but that was bordering into some pretty gray territory and we weren't really looking to move past selfies into full-blown photo-ops. We were juggling three or four politically based offers at the time including those from Topeka, the capital of Kansas, and Jefferson City, the capital of Missouri, but we all felt that any local politics should stay out of the Sungwoo tour. Then they offered to sweeten the pot a bit.

They offered to have former Royal Frank White there to give Sungwoo the gift. The whole thing reeked of politics, but one of Sungwoo's favorite Royals was Frank White.

White, himself, is a fascinating figure in Royals history. He was on the construction crew that literally poured the foundation concrete for the Truman Sports Complex — better known as Kauffman and Arrowhead Stadiums. He was a member of the Royals Baseball Academy — a before-its-time instructional program that graduated White as well as Rangers manager Ron Washington. He went on to be one of the greatest second basemen NOT in the Baseball Hall of Fame, ending his career with 160 homers, 2006 hits and countless images from my youth of him jumping into the air to turn a double-play. His number 20 is one of only three numbers retired by the Royals, and he played 2,324 games in the Major Leagues — all as a member of his hometown Royals.

Following his playing career, he became an instructor and minor league manager throughout the 1990s. He managed current Royals including Alex Gordon, Billy Butler and Eric Hosmer. To White, he felt he was paying his dues to someday take over as manager of the Royals (or "Rawls," if you hear him talk.)

But he was passed over at least three times for managerial positions, only ever becoming a base coach for the big league team.

He also was a popular broadcaster for television, but enough was enough, and he famously quit the franchise he dedicated his life to and vowed never to return to Kauffman Stadium.

In the past several years, White has been a coach for the Independent Minor League Kansas City T-Bones in Kansas City, Kansas, and most recently has run for public office with the Jackson County Legislature. This is where we pick up the Jackson County story.

White's involvement with Sungwoo wasn't a slam-dunk though, simply because he was running for the legislature and had not yet been elected. Allowing White to present Sungwoo with the proclamation might poison the election. In the end, White was ultimately allowed to stand in the chamber and present Sungwoo with a signed number 20 jersey while County Legislator Mike Sanders presented Sungwoo with the decree. Sungwoo was so happy, he gave White one of his now signature bear hugs. He wore the signed jersey out of the building as we headed to Kauffman Stadium as guests of the Royals to watch their batting practice.

Sungwoo receives a proclamation from Jackson County Chairman Scott Burnett and former Royals second baseman (and future Jackson County Councilman) Frank White

The hugs were flowing freely now as a visibly giddy Sungwoo was suffering from both a week of jet lag as well as nervousness about tonight's first pitch. But he was attacking it like a punch-drunk boxer throwing out hugs as he stood on the field for Royals batting practice. Hugs went out to Alex Gordon, Lorenzo Cain and the man who promised to fly him to the United States, Danny Duffy. Duffy presented Sungwoo with signed cleats, a jersey and a hat.

Sungwoo was also on the pregame show where former Royal Jeff Montgomery presented him with a signed glove. We tried to figure up the value of the swag that Sungwoo received just that day and it kept totaling up to priceless numbers.

Sungwoo kept fidgeting, though, and as happy as he was to finally meet his heroes, he was still very, very nervous. "I don't want to ruin it all," he told me — somehow equating a poor first pitch to a house of cards of events that would all crash to the ground if he buried his ceremonial pitch short.

Sungwoo warms up moments before the first pitch at Kauffman Stadium (photo by Bob Niffen)

Once again he was warming up for a pitch — this time in the bowels of the stadium in a service tunnel behind the Royals dugout. Every pitch was spot on as he planned out his windup and delivery. Three... four... ten... twenty pitches... all perfect strikes, and then the events lady said firmly... "It's time."

Onto the field he walked to a large applause that is normally reserved for the starting lineups. He strode atop the mound and then made a James Shields-like bow and turn toward first base in order to hold a phantom runner.

In the pantheon of ceremonial first pitches, there are good ones, there are bad ones. The bad ones nearly always fall short. The mound is only 60 feet, six inches from home, but the first time you stand on a mound in a Major League stadium, it's extremely intimidating and the plate looks like it's 12 miles away. So the entire day, we'd been telling him, "just don't skip it."

Well, he didn't skip it. In fact, his throw caught some major air and sailed over the head of Ethan Bryan, a local author who Sungwoo chose to be the catcher. Bryan was unable to leap high enough and the throw sailed to the backstop, allowing the phantom runner on first to easily make it to second.

Sungwoo was mortified and walked off the field looking ashen and depressed.

To us, it was simply a throw that slipped out of the hand. To Sungwoo, it was the end of the run of luck. Maybe the fans would start to boo. Maybe the fans would throw things. Maybe people back home would see and those late-night insensitive tweets would be right. Maybe the team would laugh. Or worse, maybe the team would start losing.

It wasn't looking good for the Boys in Blue. The Royals were tied with the Oakland Athletics, a team that was also looking for the postseason, 2–2 going into the seventh inning. Sungwoo spent the first few innings in his seats donated to him by 610 Sports but was really lacking the energy and enthusiasm of the previous couple of days.

So by the sixth inning, we did what most other Royals fans do to calm the nerves: we stepped up to the bar. We found our newest, dearest friend Elizabeth, a lab tech at Boulevard Brewing, and cozied up at the Boulevard stand behind home plate. Sungwoo and I started tipping them back. The private tour of the brewery we got earlier in the trip proved that Sungwoo knew his beers, but this wasn't a light night — this was some drinking to quell the anger he had inside. He felt he had brought great shame on himself and the Royals by sailing the first pitch, and nothing but Boulevard Pale Ale was going to make him forget.

The bar is set back far enough to where you need to rely on the television screens to watch the game, and I glanced up to find Nori Aoki standing on second base in the bottom of the seventh with two outs.

Alcides Escobar, the shortstop for the Royals, is a fascinating study in the power of positive thinking. During the entire 2012 and 2013 seasons, crotchety and hard-headed Ned Yost insisted in leaving the weak-hitting shortstop in games late for two reasons. One, his defense is other-worldly. He could save a game just with his glove, and removing him for offense makes your team worse. Secondly, he wanted to let Escobar experience moments late in games to get ready for them later in his career.

This was one of those moments. Athletics pitcher Sonny Gray had pitched six and two-thirds innings of two-run baseball against the hottest team in the American league, but left a pitch out over the plate for Escobar, who slapped it right back up the middle to score Aoki from second. The Royals were ahead 3–2.

Even then, Sungwoo's attitude was only mildly improved. The beer helped, as did Escobar's single, but it wasn't until my phone rang that the trip went from incredible to unbelievable.

"Hey Chris, are you guys still here?" The woman on the other end of the cell phone call was Erin Sleddens, a member of the Royals marketing staff. "We were kind of wondering, would Sungwoo like to hang the 'W'?"

So, the "W" was a relatively new tradition that was only started at the beginning of the season by the folks with the Hall of Fame in left field. The idea is lifted from the Chicago Cubs, who would fly a "W" flag prior to the days of radio and television, so folks on the L train would know if the Cubs won on their way home from work. Curt Nelson and Dave Webster are the men behind the corny idea in Kansas City, and prior to August 11, 2014, I thought the idea was stupid. That is no longer my thought.

"Yes. Absolutely." I said as I began to tremble.

"Come to the Hall of Fame as soon as you can."

I whispered into Elizabeth's ear what was about to happen and she began to shake with excitement.

"Sungwoo, the Royals would like you to hang the W if we hold onto the lead."

"On the Hall of Fame? The W?" And the smile returned. The color rushed back into his face and we both darted down the concourse, once again pausing for about 20 selfies on the way.

As we made it to the front doors of the Hall, the game was already in the bottom of the eighth. The building that houses the Hall of Fame shuts down to the public after the seventh inning, so we knocked on the door and were greeted by the curator, Curt Nelson. "I'm so glad you made it. Come on. Hurry."

I accompanied him through the now dimly lit exhibition area. There was the 1985 World Series trophy glowing alongside a gigantic "5" made up of 3,000 baseballs signifying George Brett's 3,000th hit. But there was no time for browsing. Curt and Dave rapidly led us to the back of the building, to a small little closet.

"Okay, now start climbing." Dave pointed Sungwoo and me to a small auxiliary ladder that went up a level.

It was midway up the second of three terrifyingly narrow ladders that I wondered if this might have been a horrible mistake.

Above me was KayCee (Dave), dressed in a period wool baseball uniform/costume, below him was Sungwoo. Next in this train of terror was my fat ass, and finally Curt.

So we are halfway up the second of three ladders and KayCee yells down to Curt, "Maybe we should've had them sign something, yanno, for liability." It was at that moment that I figured if the ocean didn't take me while surfing, surely I could do no worse than dying in the Royals Hall of Fame.

Of course, nobody fell. Nobody died. Sungwoo successfully climbed to the top of the third ladder, he peered through the crack in the door three stories above the Hall of Fame like some nutty "knothole gang" out of the 1930s, and I begin to weep. Of course Greg Holland notched his league-leading 35th save of the season. Of course he overcame two runners on to do it, and of course the Royals gained sole possession of first place for the first time in August in as long as I can remember.

Baseball is a religion to a lot of people out there. To those who subscribe to the Church of Baseball, the moment that followed went beyond magical directly into spiritual.

In one of the most popular game in Royals history, it was Sungwoo who helped steal the show after the game (Fox Sports Kansas City)

At the end of the final out, these two little double-doors swung open and there was Dave and Sungwoo, as if walking into the most incredible saloon. This old-timey baseball player and this South Korean. It seemed like the setup for a joke.

Dave went out first followed by Sungwoo and then mayhem. The Crown Vision video board showed Jarrod Dyson doing a standing backflip and then the next shot was of Sungwoo emerging holding the "W," jumping and pumping his fist. I was just behind with my cell phone camera rolling as well as laughing with a tired three-day Vegas road-trip voice.

The Royals were in first place and Sungwoo was screaming. "Don't fall off the fucking roof," I remember telling him, seconds before the final out was made.

The video of him holding up the "W" and velcroing it to the side of the Hall of Fame was the Clip of the Month on MLB.com and was shown the world over, including SportsCenter that night. It was chosen as the "Fan Moment of the Year" by MLB Network following the season.

The clip that wasn't shown? His airmailed first pitch.

Chapter 13
The Coach

The Coach and his family before a recent Royals game

By Tuesday, Sungwoo had been in the country for nearly a week. Those of us who had taken vacation days were starting to head back to work. Tuesday found us with a dilemma, because of the popularity of Sungwoo and the Magical Mystery Tour he seemed to be taking all of us on. We had a full agenda but nobody left to drive him around.

Feeling that asking the generosity of the Internet for a car service for the day would be a bit too much, the task of sticking to the agenda fell to a 69-year-old baggage delivery driver from Kansas City North.

"Sure, no problem. Just tell me where to be and when to be there," Ed said when I got off the phone with him Monday night. The agenda was packed and time-locked, so I was nervous leaving a task of this magnitude for my former baseball coach.

TUESDAY 8/12 AGENDA

11:30 a.m. – Lunch with Billy Butler at Zarda BBQ

2 p.m. – Meet Mayor Sly James at City Hall

3:30 p.m. – Book shopping on Plaza

6 p.m. – Dinner in Crown Club at Kauffman Stadium

7 p.m. – Royals vs. Oakland (Crown Seats) (Loss 1-3)

I was at work, but constantly texting his phone. He hadn't yet learned to text back anything other than "k" so I had to angle my text messages towards k-friendly responses.

"You're on the road to City Hall, right?"

"k"

"Meeting the Mayor went okay?"

"k"

"Made it to Zarda? Is Billy Butler there?"

"k"

My meetings that day slowed to a crawl and conference calls seemed to never end.

I don't know why I doubted him, yet there I was, every three minutes, looking at the clock and fearing that faith was misguided. Ed had never let me down, not a single time I'd felt like this, but there I was.

For decades, Ed had managed to take care of the baseball dreams for not only me, but also thousands of children in the Kansas City Northland. My first baseball coach volunteered when nobody else would commit. He worked late, came early and coached me and my brother through our formative baseball years. But that's not where he stopped. When the health of League Director A.J. Wilson started to fail, Ed ran for the Board of Directors for the North Kansas City Area Baseball Association and was named League Director a few years later. For the next 20 years, Ed worked every day at two northland ballparks: A.J. Wilson Sports Complex, named after his predecessor, as well as Water Well Park, a park he worked with the city to design and maintain.

One of my first summer jobs was at Water Well as the groundskeeper the first years the park opened. When the Great Flood of 1993 threatened the park, which sat at the banks of the Missouri River, Ed and I hopped in a canoe to paddle to a submerged concession stand to save a popcorn machine and in-ground bases, which were now floating away and threatening to become the property of Columbia or St. Louis, further downriver.

Ed spent every night patrolling the parks either as the director, a coach, or even a substitute umpire, oftentimes signalling "out" with a thumb in the air (much to my chagrin). But he still managed to work tirelessly for decades and keep a twinkle in his eye.

One October in the mid-1990s, we were laying out new sod for one of the fields and Ed drove by to check on the progress. He taught me that the most important part of laying sod is that the "green side always has to go up." But in his defense, he wasn't really working with seasoned professionals.

Another morning, Ed drove up to find me and my friend Craig sitting in the groundskeeper's shack playing cards after it rained. The clouds had all burned off and we were simply waiting for the day's games to be cancelled. All of the field lights in the park were on, which set Ed off. "What in the hell are you guys doing sitting on your ass and why are all the god-damned lights on?" My friend Craig looked at him with a straight face and said, "We were waiting for the lights to dry the field." Ed looked at him with a blank stare and walked away mumbling under his breath.

His skin was the shade of someone of a more southern locale — permanently tanned by the sun after hours of dragging fields and setting out bases and mowing criss-crosses into the turf. He was never without his signature 44-ounce Coca-Cola and a pack of smokes, a fact that Sungwoo, the child of a father struggling with lung cancer, wouldn't let him forget.

We would get into arguments nearly every summer, often times with me stomping off and quitting only to come back the next day early to fill up the gasoline cans and start on the mowing and field preparation work. Those hot summer days were hell on your attitude. But everything he ever asked for or did was for the kids of the Northland — so that they could have baseball in their lives. He spoke often of how baseball and team sports were the keys to teaching kids to stay off the streets and lead a good life. But his attention to detail was well known and hard to ever get completely right.

A couple of years ago, Ed was honored by the league for 30 years of service with a street sign at the opening drive of A.J. Wilson Sports Complex, and it still hangs there today.

But in the back of my mind, I was still very nervous to turn over driving responsibility for this international star to my old baseball coach. I also knew that he should somehow be a part of this — just as he'd been a part of baseball for thousands of kids across the decades.

He hit every timeline and got to stand in the chambers of the Mayor of Kansas City, Sly James, as Sungwoo and the Mayor toured the balcony atop City Hall. He got to grab a cup of coffee and have a long conversation with Sungwoo at a coffee shop in the historic City Market and tell some stories about how the city has grown and changed over the years since he grew up in Kansas City, Kansas's Strawberry Hill Polish district.

They even added pitstops along the way — something that I only found out later as I likely would not have approved. They stopped at a bookstore on the Plaza and Sungwoo walked away with four or five books about Royals baseball, its history, the Negro Leagues and the 1985 World Series. Ed and Sungwoo talked about everything Ed had seen related to baseball as he grew up through the eras of the Athletics and the Royals.

They made it to the east side of town, where a special lunch was set up between Sungwoo and Royals designated hitter Billy Butler over some Zarda BBQ as a fundraising event for Butler's Hit-It-A-Ton foundation. And he even made it back to get Sungwoo to the baseball game that night.

On that Tuesday, as he chaperoned Sungwoo around, he hit all the stops perfectly. The whirlwind Sungwoo tour simply wouldn't have been the same without Ed. Without my dad, Ed Kamler. The sign that is at the opening of the park? It says "Kamler's Way," which seems fitting on a number of levels.

In the words of my father, that whole day was "K."

Chapter 14

The Rest & The Roof

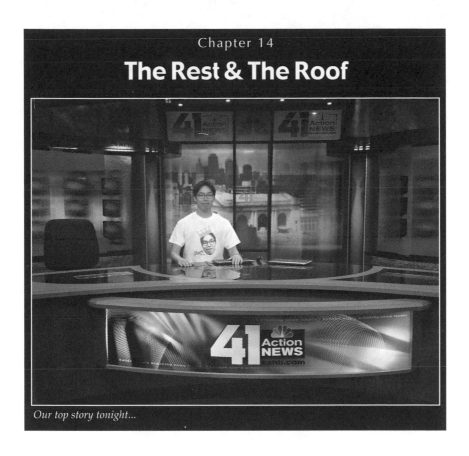

Our top story tonight...

Somebody on Twitter said it pretty well towards the end of Sungwoo's trip. "This is starting to feel like your third day in Vegas."

We were on an insane pace, and we only had one more day to go. We watched the first loss of Sungwoo's trip on Tuesday night from the Crown Seats thanks to an extremely generous anonymous donation from someone who was enjoying watching Sungwoo experience Kansas City. I woke up to a private message on Twitter explaining that there were four Crown Seats waiting for us at will call, as well as some gift cards for souvenirs.

That same anonymous person ended up kicking in a significant sum for the Kickstarter fundraiser for this book. Whoever you are... thank you.

The downside is that we did see a loss. The Royals got crushed, and part of me was kind of glad the bubble had finally burst.

Dave Darby took him around his final full day in Kansas City and they met with a reporter from the *New Yorker* magazine, who was doing a story. You know. Just your regular Wednesday morning.

WEDNESDAY AND THURSDAY 8/13-14 AGENDA

10 a.m. - Meet with New Yorker Reporter

Noon - Lunch at Nick & Jakes on Main

4 p.m. - Appearance at KSHB Channel 41

7 p.m. - Royals vs. Oakland (Win 3-0)

10 p.m. - Sungwoo crash on our couch

2 a.m. - Leave for Airport

4:30 a.m. - Flight to San Francisco - KCI Terminal C

The bittersweet ending happened at The K that night when we saw the Royals get back on their winning ways against the Athletics 3-0. I got to show Sungwoo how to keep score in a scorebook — a moment I will never ever forget.

There were a million little moments over those ten days that could fill 30 books. Kind gestures by people. Photographs that we took. Places we went. Everyone who just wanted to say thank you for coming to Kansas City.

Most likely my favorite was on the first full day he was in town. We had done the BBQ in the morning and the radio interview, and then we got a tour of Boulevard Brewery by Elizabeth Belden.

You can sign up for tours of the facility and hundreds of people do on the weekends. It's really a madhouse. The whole story of Boulevard is fascinating and a real success story of Kansas City. The other side of the coin is the love that is shared by Kansas Citians to one of their own. Budweiser is "St. Louis's beer." Boulevard belongs to Kansas City — even though it is smaller and less popular, it is ours. And the love of people on Twitter for some of their smaller seasonal craft beers is Beatles-like. (Seriously. Just search Twitter for #ChocolateAle and sit back and marvel.)

Sungwoo significantly improved his knowledge of Kansas City beer while in Kansas City, one Tank 7 at a time.

It's a story of someone accomplishing something modestly and humbly. And it really reflects Sungwoo's story here in Kansas City. This is a guy who was just a baseball fan. He wanted to pay homage to the team he'd followed from afar for 20 years. But Kansas City loves that kind of story. They love it with a capital "L."

So here we were getting this private tour of the factory. It was late and folks were heading home after a long day. But Elizabeth stuck around to show off her expansive knowledge of beer and also to just spend some time with the Committee (of which she is now a card-carrying member).

Sungwoo and Elizabeth hit it off in a cosmic sort of sense. They talked about beer for an hour. I'm not a huge beer guy, so my eyes kind of rolled back in my head, but we were in one of their tasting rooms and the beer was free so I wasn't complaining.

They kept talking about the different ingredients and the flavors and tastes and Sungwoo was loving it. He was used to drinking lager beers, as that was all that was available for many decades folowing the war and by the oligopoly Korean beer industry. There was even talk after tipping a few back of opening a Boulevard franchise in Seoul. So look for that coming when we all win the lottery.

But the moment I'll likely never forget was as we went up to the roof of this three-story building in the Southwest Boulevard area of town, just outside of the downtown loop — an industrial area surrounded by some of the best Mexican restaurants in the region.

The roof of Boulevard Brewery has been turned into some sort of natural reclamation meant to "green" the area. There was soil and grass and plants growing, and it looked like a very Zen-type place. It is not open to the public but meant for employees and special guests to visit for short periods of time.

But the view. The view is a side of Kansas City I'd never seen. It overlooks the Kauffman Center for the Performing Arts, the sculptures above Bartle Hall and the skyscrapers of downtown, and to the right is the Liberty Memorial.

On top of the Boulevard Brewing Company roof (left to right) Jeff Huerter, myself, Lee Sungwoo and Elizabeth Belden

There was a storm rolling in from the west. A good looking storm, too. One with a lot of lightning that was fast moving. It also was coming at sunset so it had the deep purples and greens that only folks in the Midwest know about. People from the West Coast that I talk to sometimes ask me about thunderstorms. I tell them that we sit on our front porches and watch them roll in. They tell me I'm crazy. But if you ever see those colors and that majesty — you'd know I was right.

So we're just watching all of it. The lightning. The buildings. The I-35 rush hour traffic roll by. My eyes started to water. It happened maybe a dozen times while Sungwoo was in town. I'm not a cryer. I'm not a sappy kind of guy. But there I was. Watching my city from an angle I'd never seen it before. And I realized that Kansas City is not just a six-sided die, but it's an infinitely-sided die and I got to see nearly every side of it over that week because of Sungwoo.

I stood on the roof of Boulevard Brewery in the middle of a rainstorm with friends who are now friends forever and listened to the silence.

Chapter 15
The Run

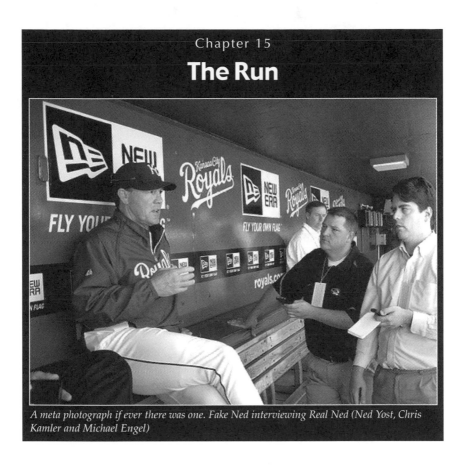

A meta photograph if ever there was one. Fake Ned interviewing Real Ned (Ned Yost, Chris Kamler and Michael Engel)

Ned Yost is a genius. There. I said it. It's in a book. So now it's true. He is. He's a genius. What is his special genius skill? The ability to do nothing and let issues wash over him.

I first saw this special superpower in action with my Grandpa Kamler. He was hard of hearing and later passed away due to Alzheimer's. Every Friday, Mom and Dad would pile us into the station wagon and take us up to Strawberry Hill in Kansas City, Kansas, to let Grandma and Grandpa watch us while the parents went to their bowling league.

We'd spend the evening watching *Knight Rider* or *Love Boat* and eat Grandma's famous fried chicken. But mostly we laughed at the way Grandma and Grandpa interacted with each other. Now. There's a big different between couples who fight and couples who have been married 50 years "interacting" with each other. The volume might be the same. The tone may feel the same. But the root of it was always love. Mostly.

> "Charlie!! Turn that TV down, you're making these
> kids deaf!!"
> <Grandpa wouldn't do anything.>
> "Charlie!! I'm not going to tell you again!!"
> <Grandpa would still do nothing.>
> "CHARLIE!!!"

Grandpa would yell back, "I can't hear you!!" And then he'd look at me and wink. I honestly think he just did most of what he did to be bullheaded and onery. A special form of entertainment.

He was constantly ripping me for being left-handed, too. Said I couldn't play checkers because it was a right-handed only set or that I can't write with a right-handed pen. He had to go get me a left-handed pen. Of course, I ate it all up.

But there's a fine line between bullheaded and stoic. And I see a lot of my Grandpa Kamler in Ned Yost and the way he managed from August 2014 on.

Over the past several seasons, he has insisted on maintaining consistent roles with his players — even in the wake of massive failures. His handling of Mike Moustakas through the entire 2014 season is the best example. Moustakas had a dreadful offensive year. Yost knew that sending him down to the minors meant not only a hit defensively, but they also didn't really have anybody tearing the cover off the ball at third base in Omaha.

Additionally, Moustakas has always been a guy who let outside influences get in his head, so a demotion was a last straw. He hit at or near .200 (the Mendoza line) for much of the season and simply couldn't stop popping up to third. When asked about Moustakas, Yost simply said it will all start clicking. A slow start and as early as May 1, there were torches being lit to send him down to the minor leagues. It didn't happen until the end of May and only for about a week. From that point on, he was really no better offensively, but Yost continued to show confidence in him every time he could.

Outside objections simply didn't faze Yost, and he allowed the team to settle on its own, relying heavily on clubhouse leadership from James Shields and Alex Gordon.

When several players got into a public spat with a local radio station and the bar owned by that station — the 810 Zone — in June, Yost mostly stayed out of it and the issue blew over. Was that inaction? Or was that letting the players resolve it on their own?

In years past, you'd have seen the clubhouse fall apart. There were notoriously bad seeds in previous Royals clubhouses. Jose Guillen, for one, was a disaster. Manager Trey Hillman was impotent against his attitude, yet his inaction led to his losing the clubhouse.

One key to 2014's success is that the clubhouse had better leaders in Shields, Guthrie and Gordon, and they had a spark.

Lee Sungwoo.

On Tuesday, August 5, the Royals were five games out of first place and Sungwoo was receiving an apple pie at All-Star Pizza in the Northland. That night, Danny Duffy struck out seven batters through five innings as the Royals crushed the lowly Arizona Diamondbacks 12–2. They won their next six games and sat only a half game out of first, as the Detroit Tigers had their own dog-day fade that coincided with the Royals streak.

The Royals started Sungwoo's trip at 58–53, a respectable five games above .500, but by no means world-beating. They would find themselves in first place when he boarded the plane back to Seoul, and they went on to lose only five more games until the final week of August. (That's really good.)

The streak began with a sense of believing. Whether it was a stoic manager believing in Mike Moustakas. Whether it was belief that the team always could prevail but just needed a spark from a far-off land. Or whether it was just the often-criticized sports phrase of capturing lightning in a bottle — this team took off on August 5 and never looked back.

The postseason was clinched on a chilly Friday night in Chicago. Several hundred fans travelled to see it in person. A few hundred others travelled to Kelly's Bar in Westport to celebrate. As the final out was made and champagne sprayed, fans everywhere cheered - the twenty-nine year curse was over.

My Grandpa Kamler used to fix old typewriters back in the 1960s and 1970s. In the basement after he passed away, we found dozens of old front-striking typewriters that were in various states of repair. Then we found one case in nearly pristine condition with a typewriter that looked brand new. We figured that he took parts and pieces from all the other typewriters as he used his experiences and knowledge to make one amazingly pristine mechanism. I think Ned Yost and my Grandpa would've gotten along very nicely.

Chapter 16

The Wild Card

Alex Robinson, Rany Jazayerli and me. Wild Cards all.

In early September, there was actually a movie studio interested in making a movie about Sungwoo and his trip to Kansas City. Two of them, in fact. I first heard about the plans in mid-September. "Sure would make a better movie, though, if they made the playoffs and popped some champagne," the movie guy told me.

On the face of it, making a movie about incredible events is a no-brainer. But movies have to be believable and have some level of reality tied to them.

It is my staunch belief that any hopes of making a Sungwoo movie were dashed because of the events of September 30, 2014. Nobody would ever believe it.

The Royals had played themselves into the American League Wild Card game against the Oakland A's. The irony of all ironies is that the game was considered part of the postseason yet played on the final day of September, so the loser couldn't even say they played in October.

With Sungwoo back in South Korea, I had to find other partners in crime to attend the game. Not attending the first postseason game in 29 years simply wasn't an option. The opportunity presented itself because of a pretty special guy in his own right, Alex Robinson. Alex works for Major League Baseball in New York as part of the Advanced Media team that runs the MLB.com website and its social media enterprises. If it sounds like it's a cool job, that's because it is.

Alex and I met the day Sungwoo toured Kauffman Stadium for the first time where he was dispatched to write an article for Cut-4, a blog-style section of MLB.com. He wrote a really cool article about Sungwoo, got some pictures and went back to New York. He emailed me a few weeks later saying how he wanted a few of the Sungwoo shirts we made to help the Bishop Sullivan Center, so I sent a few along with the strict guidelines that he photograph some hot chicks wearing them. He obliged.

But as with so many of the media folks we met that week, it was a done deal and I went back to my life. Until Alex sent me a message on Twitter. "What are you doing tonight?"

Alex explained that he had to be back in Kansas City to see the first postseason game there in 29 years and he was going to take his dad. "That's great, man. But what does this have to do with me?"

"I want you and Rany to go, too."

Rany Jazayerli is a pretty big deal amongst baseball fans – especially those that follow their teams online. I met Rany, naturally, through Twitter. We had traded jabs and snarky-spirited comments about this or that, but our friendship certainly didn't blossom until the night of the Wild Card game. Rany's origin story is amazing in and of itself. By day, Dr. Jazayerli is a dermatologist in Chicago. By night, on weekends and an occasional lunch break, he is a baseball writer for Grantland.com and a founder of *Baseball Prospectus*, the yearly annal of baseball statistical knowledge — what you'd get if *The Baseball Encyclopedia* took steroids and had a dose of personality injected as well. But he started as a Royals fan with a website "Rob and Rany on the Royals" with another baseball writer, Rob Neyer. He famously fell out of love with the team several times. Decades of poor decision making, inept play and no meaningful effort to em-brace the changing economics of baseball forced him to write this in 2009:

> *I've spent my entire adolescent and adult life rooting for and writing about this team, and it's been two decades of unrequited love. I've got too much to be thankful for in my life to let it be spoiled by the imperious decisions of a front office that looks down upon the very idea of the statistical analysis that I've advocated for so many years, and that has contributed to the success of so many other teams.*

So here we were, basically three strangers who had only known each other through Twitter, and Alex's poor, poor dad who didn't know any of us — sitting behind the third base dugout in some pretty sweet MLB seats awaiting the first pitch of Kansas City playoff baseball in over 10,000 days.

I turned to Alex and thanked him for the 200th time and then said confidently, "This is either going to be the greatest night of our lives or the worst."

What do you do when you sit at a baseball game next to a man who works for MLB and a national baseball writer? Do you talk about ways to improve the game through new technologies? Do you talk about the rising salaries and how instant replay is affecting the pace of play? Do you talk about fixing Hall of Fame voting or reducing performance enhancing drugs in sports?

Nope. You talk shit. Lots of shit.

It was basically a live version of Twitter during a Royals game — except with way more emotional swings and smack talk from 12-year-olds. Also there was dancing — but I'll get to that. The crowd was unlike any crowd I've ever seen before or since. There was just an electric hum through it, even during stoppages in play. We might not've sat down but twice during the entire game, which stretched well into the evening.

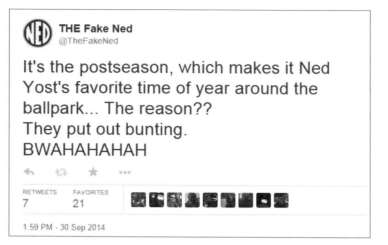

The game started off with a bitter pill as Brandon Moss hit a two-run homer in the top of the first before many had even sat down. "Welp guys, I guess this might be the worst night of our lives."

The 29 years between playoff games was an inconceivable length of time. But it hit me — hard — standing in Section 116 behind the third base dugout on that Tuesday night. It hit me that I will have watched the last two playoff games in Royals history — separated by a scant 10,565 days. But there's no way the game could live up to the hype, and the two-run first inning homer off of James Shields confirmed it.

The sinking feeling in my stomach was all too familiar. You could sense it, too. You could sense it in the over-capacity crowd of 40,502 fans jammed into every nook and cranny of Kauffman Stadium. It was nervous excitement — like when you're waiting to take finals at school. All you can do is wait and watch. And cheer. The crowd was so loud and so frenzied. At times all we could do was cheer.

But then in the bottom of the inning, Billy Butler scored Nori Aoki on a single, and we were only trailing 2-1.

The Royals took the lead in the third inning as I was frantically trying to get Sungwoo to Skype with us from the stadium, but the WiFi was overloaded because of the capacity crowd and I was too far away from the press box to steal their signal.

From an early age, I learned about sports disappointment and its close relationship with Kansas City. One of my earliest memories was crying on the brown shag carpeting when I was only four years old after the Chris Chambliss homer downed the Royals in the 1976 ALCS. It was a scar that was then layered by dozens of other scars throughout my life. The 5th Down game. Tyus Edney. Neifi Perez. Brian Anderson pitching every day we had tickets to a Royals game and getting shelled. Luke Hochevar on opening day down a million runs before anybody even sat down. Lin Elliot. These names and memories grafted over every other scab beneath.

However, The Royals were shockingly good anytime they had a lead this season. Especially in games where they scored four or more runs. As late as July, the Royals were 44-8 when scoring four runs or more and only 9-43 scoring less. But the bullpen allows to forget all those years when I can recall specific instances when Ricky "Blow"-tallico or Macdougal or Broxton coughing up leads late in the game.

Ned Yost had managed pretty poorly, frankly, through September. He got into a pissing contest of some sort with Billy Butler, benching him much of the month, and many in the media, myself included, wondered if he was going to repeat his flop of 2006 when, as manager of the Milwaukee Brewers, he lost a lead in the division and was fired two weeks before the playoffs.

#YOSTED was the hashtag originally coined by Fake Ned on Twitter to describe something monumentally Ned-like to lose a game. Baseball managers are built for such criticism yet do little to auto-correct.

James Shields had only allowed two runs when he came out for the sixth inning and immediately let two runners get on.

The whispering between Rany, Alex and myself was that surely Yost could go to relief pitcher Kelvin Herrera early here and make an exception to his "seventh inning guy" rule. Surely he could use him in the sixth if the need arose.

Instead, Yost called upon rookie pitcher Yordano Ventura. Ventura is flat nasty with a fireballing fastball. He also has an incredible change-up, which is still in the nineties but looks like a VW Beetle against the 103 MPH heater. Yost's decision to go with the rookie in this situation, a right-hand pitcher who had only three other relief appearances in his career, especially with two runners on and Brandon Moss, a left-hander, at the plate was at best a head-scratcher.

Rany, who is the king of second-guessing, actually swallowed his contempt for the decision until Moss ate the 96-mile-an-hour fastball like he was plunging into an Oklahoma Joe's Z-Man. It went… fast. Over the centerfield wall. The crowd slumped in their barely used seats. Limp. Lifeless. Another scar on top of so many others.

THE Fake Ned @TheFakeNed · Sep 30
Ned booed lustily by the capacity crowd.
11   25

THE Fake Ned @TheFakeNed · Sep 30
I feel sick.
18   33

THE Fake Ned @TheFakeNed · Sep 30
Ned.
7   19

THE Fake Ned @TheFakeNed · Sep 30
Ventura is up.
1   3

Baseball Reference, a wonderful website for baseball nerds, had the win expectancy for the Royals at 67% when the sixth inning started and then swung it around to the A's at 73% after the Moss homer.

The crowd was still. Rany was turning purple. Ever the long-form writer, he was rapidly tapping notes into his iPhone for a rant of epic proportions upon conclusion of the game. A game that almost certainly would end with the Royals failing to make it to October in their first postseason performance in 29 years.

Jon Lester barreled through the lifeless Royals in the sixth and seventh. The discussion between Alex, Rany and myself at that point was how small a flag would be mounted to the top of the Hall of Fame to reference the three hours of postseason baseball the Royals had appeared in. We settled on one of those little triangle felt pennants that you buy in the gift shop.

But today was somehow different. Nobody let losing the lead get to them. Nobody seemed resigned to the fact that after 29 years we'd only play playoff baseball in September. We all seemed... confident? Trailing 7-3 in the eighth inning of a winner-take-all game, we didn't seem to be sweating... much.

And then my phone buzzed. It was Sungwoo.

"Unable to get to Skype. But wanted to say don't give up."

Wut.

The eighth inning brought a barrage of singles and stolen bases so rapidly that the crowd noise was at a constant level ten for 30 minutes. Even down by four runs, I didn't see more than five empty seats in the entire stadium. The eighth inning rewarded us for sticking around as the Royals scored three in the bottom of the frame to make it 7-6, but Omar Infante stranded Alex Gordon on second base to take it to the ninth inning still down a run.

Josh Willingham led off the ninth with a single and yielded to pinch runner Jarrod Dyson. I interviewed Dyson earlier in the year in the clubhouse and he didn't lift his head above his iPad while playing *Clash of Clans*. We talked for several minutes about him being at level 87 and how he was addicted to the game. Royals coach Rusty Kuntz — who himself has been ripe for jabs by Fake Ned — had to literally talk Dyson out of playing the game to focus on baseball. Now he was called upon to pinch run to save the season.

He immediately advanced to second on an Escobar sac bunt and then stole third. Man on third, one out for Nori Aoki, who sacrifice flied the *Clash of Clans* player home from third to tie the game and bring the crowd noise to an 87 on a scale of 1-10.

New ballgame. Free baseball. The Royals were still fighting to make it to October. Sungwoo's text came through. We never gave up.

From the moment the tenth inning started, there was just this sensation buzzing throughout the crowd. Maybe this really was destiny. Maybe there was absolutely no way this team could lose. Maybe this was it.

And then a seeing-eye single in the top of the twelfth inning by former Royal Alberto Callaspo scored the go-ahead run for the A's. It was twenty minutes until midnight. Twenty minutes until October. I tweeted that the irony of all of this was that the Royals wouldn't make it to October baseball. And then I got the text from my wife. "It's Brett. He's crying." Brett is my 12-year-old son who NEVER cries. Ever. He also rarely stays up to watch baseball, and he plays FIFA soccer on the XBox. But he was invested in this. He was all in. He was now crying. Sitting on the floor with his Royals hat on.

I was four years old all over again watching Chambliss's homer sail into the seats at Yankee Stadium. My son now had his first deep cut from Kansas City sports. He has skin in the game now. The Royals were trailing 8-7 heading to the bottom of the 12th. I thought about what Sungwoo might've said in this moment and I texted back to my wife, "Don't let him go to bed yet. We've still got three outs."

The only things the Royals had going for them at this point were the home-field advantage and the hope that the Royals could come back a third time in this game. Completely improbable — but what about this run since Sungwoo arrived in August hadn't been improbable?

There's always some guy at the end of a bar who will tell you the following phrase: "I called it." There's always someone that will say he called Lin Elliott shanking the field goal against the Colts in 1993. There's always some guy who said he called Don Denkinger's famous blown call in Game 5 of the 1985 World Series. There's always one guy who called that Sporting KC would go to penalty kicks on a frigid October night to win the MLS Cup in 2013.

But I'm here to tell you that I called the bottom of the 12th inning.

I turned to my now dear friend Alex — the man whose seat I was occupying and who over the course of the past four hours I had drunk with and laughed with and hugged and cried with — and I uttered the following phrase: "You're about to see something incredible."

"Bullshit," he told me. "But I like where your heart is at."

The crowd, down 8-7, was still very much into the game and nobody had left. But it was an extremely nervous energy now pulsing through The K.

In the eighth inning, these Royals, who had only the weapons of pitching and speed left, had refused to die. A LET'S GO ROYALS chant rose from the upper deck. It filtered to the lower levels. Then stolen bases happened. Then Brandon Finnegan happened. We were talking in the stands about "what's the craziest thing that could ever happen?" and then something crazier would happen. Illogical pinch hitters. Steals of third. Coming back late from down two. It all happened. I know that it happened. I saw it. But I do not believe it. Ned Yost was the crazy uncle at Thanksgiving that climbs up on the roof to pee, drives his Oldsmobile into the swimming pool, then pulls a quarter out of your ear with a wink.

By the time Lorenzo Cain stepped into the box in the bottom of the twelfth inning, all 40,000+ fans were screaming at the top of their lungs. Cain rose to the challenge by... weakly grounding out for the first out of the inning.

Despair set in. This wasn't going to happen. We had made it this far, but no farther. We wouldn't even see goddamn October baseball (although the clock was nearing midnight, so maybe we'd see a few minutes of it).

Oakland had an 89% chance of winning following the LoCain ground out.

THE Fake Ned
@TheFakeNed

We are 35 minutes from October.

Kansas City, MO

RETWEETS   FAVORITES
13   22

11:25 PM - 30 Sep 2014

Cain making an out brought to the plate Eric Hosmer. Hosmer was two different players at times this season. Himself in an adolescent period of his career. Not yet a rookie, but not yet relied on as a veteran. He worked a 2-2 count and then blasted a drive to the Kauffman Stadium night in left-center. It landed at the base of the wall thanks to a collision between Sam Fuld and Jonny Gomes. Hosmer sped into third, only 90 feet away from tying the game.

In our seats, it was off the hook. Crowd noise was never a problem that night, but it went to an even higher voltage after the triple, and the volume remained as former first-round draft choice Christian Colon drove a chopping infield single that scored a head-first diving Hos.

I looked down at my phone and it had struck midnight.

THE Fake Ned
@TheFakeNed

We made it to October.

RETWEETS   FAVORITES
61   124

12:06 AM - 1 Oct 2014

Bedlam. We had been screaming for five hours and had no voices left, yet we yelled even louder and clapped and danced and waved our towels. Stranger-hugging time had begun. High fives were dispensed to anyone and everyone near us. 89% in Oakland's favor had swung in two at bats to 63% in Kansas City's favor.

Gordon made the second out, and Colon was still on first. This prompted Salvador Perez to step into the box nursing an 0-5 night. Colon managed to steal second off of right-hander Jason Hammel on a failed pitchout and the crowd nervously maintained a steady chant of Let's Go Royals.

"This is ending right here." I leaned over to Alex. He gave me a look. The at-bat took forever as Hammel kept throwing over and checking the runner.

With Colon on second and a 2-2 count, pitch number five was up and in to Perez. But he spoiled this one to see pitch number six.

Pitch number six was never intended to be hit. It was what catchers call a "waste pitch" designed to get Perez, a notoriously poor pitch selector, to swing and maybe strike out on an unhittable ball.

The pitch was simply unhittable. Yet Perez swung at it. It was midway into the other batter's box it was so far outside. As he swung the bat, the crowd noise dropped from an 11 to a zero. Silence. Slow motion. Perez bends nearly over at the waist and slaps at the ball with such force that it blasts down the third base line past a diving Josh Donaldson. It lands inches in fair territory and is ruled fair by third base umpire Bill Welke.

Colon speeds around third and scores without a throw on the single on a waste pitch. Silence to insanity in a millisecond.

For nearly an hour, the crowd remained, myself included — slack jawed at the greatest baseball game we had ever seen.

A shared experience with 40,502 of my nearest friends and two now-lifelong friends. I looked back down at my phone, which was clinging to its final desperate percent of battery life. There was a text from my wife. "It's Brett. He's crying. But happy this time." My tears of sorrow from Chris Chambliss. My son's tears of elation from Salvador Perez.

I leaned over to Alex and said, "I told you this would be the greatest night of our lives."

Life never lives up to the hype. The rollercoaster is never worth the 90 minute wait in line. The new phone that was supposed to change your life is only moderately good, doesn't make phone calls and the battery doesn't last long enough. That new TV show is a disaster. The hype sets an unachievable bar every time.

Well... that was, until the final night of September and the wee hours of October.

The greatest baseball game in postseason history. Arguably. But it's a good argument. Those events all happened. And yet, no words can do justice to the release of cheers and elation from those 40,000+ fans, stadium workers, police officers, players and crew. It was impossible. It was unfathomable. It was pure Royals. It was Kansas City. It eclipsed the hype.

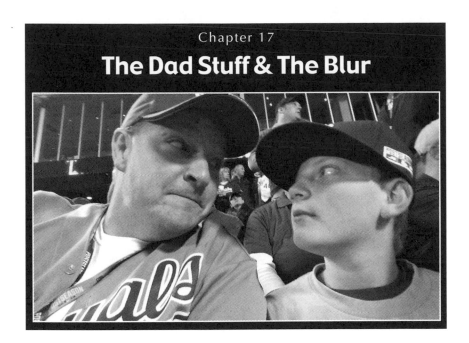

Chapter 17
The Dad Stuff & The Blur

There's just something about baseball that is unique to fathers and sons. Sons learn the game from their fathers and the fathers look to reclaim their youth teaching the sons. It is the circle of life wrapped around 108 stitches on a leather ball.

My son Brett wasn't old enough to hold his head up before one was placed in his hand. It's just part of the Kamler family heritage. Brett, named after the Royals legend, of course, had never known his hometown baseball team to be a true winner until the night of the Wild Card game.

He would go on to witness one of the greatest undefeated runs in the history of baseball. The Royals went on to win eight in a row, including his first live postseason baseball game.

Through a very gracious gift from a friend, I got to watch a post-season baseball game with my son. Even better is that I got to watch the 2014 Kansas City Royals *with* him. It's always special to watch October baseball in person. The crowd, the energy and the passion are heightened with each pitch — but nobody here in town who saw it will deny that this was even more special with *how* they did it.

The Royals were playing as children. They were laughing. They were playing without a care, and they were clearly having fun. Their innocence was on display for everyone to see.

In the second inning of ALCS Game 3, Eric Hosmer made an awkward stop on a grounder to his right. Hosmer, always the first baseman to take the play by himself, shooed Jeremy Guthrie away and dove head first into first base to record the force out. My son, a first baseman who wears No. 35 (Hosmer's number) on his back, was screaming, "I DO THAT!! I DO THAT!!" And he does. Brett has a flair for the dramatic and likes to take plays solo — often at great risk to his fielding percentage. He absolutely recognized his muse as Hosmer dove into first. Brett was living and dying with every pitch.

Brett is also reaching that age where the world is becoming much less innocent. He's in middle school now, which means pressure from peers, and he pays attention to what socks he's going to wear and even how he should wear his backpack as he walks through the halls. This attention to detail is comical for a 42-year-old, but it's the difference between success and failure to a middle schooler. He is concerned about his grades nearly as much as he is concerned with his Call of Duty scores. He's growing up.

It is this time in Brett's life where it becomes even more important for a father to teach the lessons of baseball to the son, and the October Royals provide an excellent textbook.

- Never Quit – This team was counted out dozens of times, as recently as the beginning of September. Players were sent to the minor leagues. There is no correlation between their stats and how well they played. But nobody quit.

- Play Every Day – Not quitting also means not letting up or letting the negatives in. There's plenty of bad news in the world. It is your choice on how you work around it and keep going. It's turning #Yosted into a positive.

- Have Fun – This is really what it comes down to. There's a great debate in baseball, as there is in just about every segment of our society, on the "right way" to go about your business. Serious things are serious, of course. But that doesn't mean you can't have fun, and it also means you need to keep that level of wonderment in your life. Mike Moustakas had, statistically, one of the worst seasons by a third baseman in the history of Major League Baseball, but he got damn close to winning an MVP in the ALCS. And he did it all with a smile and a wink.

My son is moving into the age where the world gets less fun. He's going to have good days and bad days, and there will always be reasons for bad days. But at the end of the playoff game, I turned the camera around and took a four second video that I hope he will look at when the bad days are really bad — when the fun days are potentially over — if that ever happens. It was taken as the final out occurred — the final out in the seventh straight postseason victory for the Kansas City Royals in Game 3 of the ALCS. The final out that put them 27 outs from their first World Series in 29 years and in his lifetime. This is what it's all about. This is what we all need to find in ourselves, and this is the fire by which we need to live. This is the fire with which the 2014 Royals fed off of. This is what fathers pass onto their sons through baseball.

Through some sort of glitch at the hospital, I held my son before my wife moments after he was born. She was in labor for what seemed like hours and the doctor finally gave up and said he was going to go to sleep. Of course, once the doc hit maximum REM cycles, that's when Kara decided to give birth to Brett. And she did it FAST. So fast that the doctor never really made it into the room. So the nurse delivered our little boy and while they were working on Kara, they just handed me the slimy little brat I would come to know as my little brat son.

As I held this crying little ball of goo, I found myself running my fingers over his chest in a circular motion, very gently, and the baby stopped crying. When we got Brett home, we would fall asleep on the couch watching the Chiefs or the Royals. Every time, I'd make that same circular motion on his back until he fell asleep.

Through the years the dad stuff stayed rewarding. I taught him to grip a baseball. I taught him to open Angry Birds on an iPad. I taught him to not turn down the pages of a library book. You know... Dad stuff.

Dad stuff is very different from Mom stuff. The old saying goes that Dad is the one to say "no" while Mom is the one to say "yes." And for the most part that's true. Mom has the extra cookie. Mom has the extra 15 minutes to stay up. But Dad stuff is the questions. "Dad, why is the steering wheel on that side of the car?" "Dad, why is a football shaped like that?" "Dad, why can't I get past this level on Mario Brothers?" "Dad, why do girls sit down to go to the bathroom?"

As a father, I think it's my right to screw with him with those answers. "Well, son, first off, the steering wheel is like that because we won World War II. A football is the same shape as your brain. Let me show you the cheat code for Mario Brothers." And for the final question... "Go ask your mother."

But that last week in October might've been my finest fatherly moment — taking my son to a World Series game in his hometown. But being a dad is so much more than that. It's showing him how to write his name in the snow. It's showing him to respect women by only watching their butt from across the room. And it's teaching him the "child friendly" cuss words when Mike Moustakas strikes out DAG NABBIT YOU FRACKING PIECE OF SNOT!!

Dad stuff is great. And I think I'm really good at it. It's filled a part of my heart that I never knew was vacant, and he has turned into not only my son, but my best friend. Dad stuff isn't always simple, but it's always special because dads have that special power.

Dad stuff is letting him jump in the pool less than 30 minutes after he's eaten. It's telling him double entendre knock-knock jokes. Dad stuff is pulling into a vacant parking lot to see if a 12 year old can take a stab at driving a car even as you have a firm grip on the emergency brake. And Dad stuff is also picking him up from school with news that his great grandmother passed away at age 89 and while he is crying on your shoulder, it is moving your hand in a circular motion gently as he cries himself to sleep.

Nobody said Dad stuff was easy.

They didn't lose a game until Game 1 of the World Series. No team had ever swept two postseason series before in that fashion. This shouldn't have happened. I'm not sure the city knew what hit them.

For me, early October was an exercise in unfamiliarity. Like waking up with super powers but being too timid to use them. Our baseball team was playing like world beaters. Our manager was making all the right moves. Our team, known for not hitting home runs, was hitting home runs. It was all very surreal.

When I look back to the ALDS against Anaheim and the ALCS against Baltimore, I can recall only stray moments. I've never been an instant-recall sort of guy, but I can tell you nearly every moment of the Wild Card game. After that, I can recall only the Moustakas catch and a few homers for the next two weeks. Brandon Finnegan. Lorenzo Cain. A few stolen bases. Billy Butler doing the "rev me up" thing.

Frankly, the entire town was exhausted. I think we can all say that now. We were damn tired. We. Just. Kept. Winning. #FirstWorld-Problems, right?

To be on that level of nervousness and excitement and running on a few fewer hours of sleep every day takes its toll. But we were also very superstitious. I had the opportunity to go to a couple postseason games and I made sure to wear the exact same outfit each time. The outfit was undefeated. These are very real laws of the universe we are dealing with here. Now that the outfit witnessed a loss, I guess I can tell you that it was my "lucky" underpants, jeans, my blue tennis shoes, my Sungwoo shirt and my Fake Ned customized jersey.

Fun fact is that the jersey was customized at the stadium a couple years ago and actually reads FAKE NED YOST. Then, about a month later, I felt some level of remorse for having a fake account with "Yost" in the name and changed the name to THE FAKE NED, instantly making my customized jersey null and void. But I broke it out for the postseason and it made up for costing me what it cost me.

The daytime hours would be filled with Twitter boasting about the win the night before, looking ahead and cautiously boasting about the next game (and quite a bit of worrying or complaining about little things, too). Oh. And our day jobs as well. Truth be told, I should probably return my salary for October.* I was a disaster.

* I won't.

I had a coworker come by my desk. First off, let me say that my cubicle is in a fairly remote portion of my floor, which is "L" shaped. I'm in the bottom corner of the "L" and so people don't just randomly stop by my desk. She was a Cardinals fan.

Cardinals fans are the worst. They just are. Maybe that's another book I should write. *Cardinals Fans Are The Worst*, by Chris Kamler.

Anyway, I won't lay out my entire case, but I'll give you this quick story. So she comes by my desk, "Oh hey, Chris. Wow. Those Royals are something else, eh?"

"Uh. Yeah. I mean. They haven't lost a game in the postseason. So. Yeah. They're doing pretty well."

"Yeah, that's great. I'm just so happy that Royals fans get to finally experience what Cardinals fans get to go through every year."

And then I threw her out a window. The downside is that I only work on the second floor.

But you know what? She's right. She's right in a snotty sort of way. But she's still right.

We aren't bred for this. This is putting a freshwater fish into the middle of a saltwater ocean.

It was all just so unfamiliar. You would see people from ESPN driving around town. You'd have wall-to-wall Royals coverage when it should've been 100% Chiefs on the radio.

My wife took a job in September at one of the sporting goods stores near the airport. They sold t-shirts and hats and folding chairs with Royals and Missouri Tigers and Kansas Jayhawks and Chiefs. Man, she picked a crappy time to work there because a ten-hour a week job suddenly ballooned to a 35-hour a week job. She would come home and tell me about the lines out the door for anything with ROYALS on it — and even more for anything with POSTSEASON or OCTOBER on it.

It was just a magic month here in town.

I do wish I'd have stopped to smell the roses a little more through the first two full rounds of the postseason. This 8-0 run HADN'T been done before. And the other shoe never did drop (until World Series Game 7). But we all just kept grinding and wearing our lucky underwear and dancing on eggshells because we were dealing with very primal forces of nature.

It all went by in such a blur.

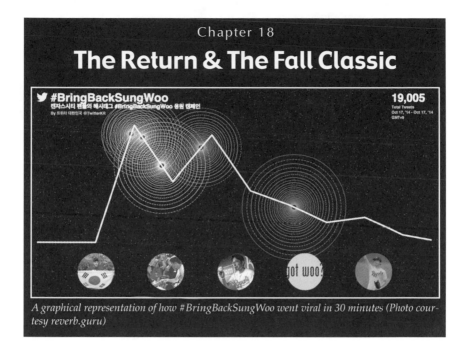

Chapter 18
The Return & The Fall Classic

🐦 #BringBackSungWoo
캔자스시티 팬들의 해시태그 #BringBackSungWoo 응원 캠페인
By 트위터 대한민국 @TwitterKR

19,005
Total Tweets
Oct 17, '14 - Oct 17, '14
GMT+9

A graphical representation of how #BringBackSungWoo went viral in 30 minutes (Photo courtesy reverb.guru)

The Committee had kept in close contact with Sungwoo since he returned to South Korea following his whirlwind visit in August. We tweeted and retweeted pictures and news articles summarizing his incredible run.

As the Royals continued to win, we would jokingly tell him, "You sure need to come back when we make the World Series!" But we knew that was impossible.

A once-in-a-lifetime event was just that. Once in a lifetime. To implore lightning to strike twice was asking too much. Sungwoo had started his new job setting up duty free stores in airports and he continued to watch over his ailing father, but he was filled with a lifetime of memories crammed into nine days as well as an apartment full of Royals baubles and trinkets — the spoils of that journey.

As the success of the team became more imminent and the Royals refused to lose in the postseason, we made a more formal pitch. I had been approached by several folks through direct messages on Twitter and email offering to fund the trip back to the United States if

Sungwoo wanted to watch the postseason. Frankly, folks just wanted to keep the thing going. But every time, Sungwoo politely declined.

The day of Game 3 of the ALCS, I got a text asking for Sungwoo's email address. This wasn't uncommon as my name had been associated with Sungwoo here stateside, so I politely obliged. The man's name was Josh Swade. He said he was a filmmaker and that he wanted to talk with Sungwoo.

I thought nothing of it and continued watching the Royals dismantle the Baltimore Orioles. But then I got a phone call from Swade outlining the crazy project he had in mind.

Swade works for Maggievision, a company that produces television. They help produce the ESPY awards for ESPN, and Swade makes documentaries. The most recent was one he sold to ESPN about the Kansas Jayhawks, the history of the game, the founder of basketball, Dr. James Naismith, and how he wanted to get the original rules written by Dr. Naismith to a museum in Lawrence, Kansas.

On our call, he described how he contacted Sungwoo and offered to fly him back to the United States for the World Series. Sungwoo politely declined, as he had done to us and several others. But Swade was unwilling to let the matter die. He described his plans to fly to South Korea personally with a camera crew and talk him into it.

He also said that the tickets had been purchased and he was leaving inside of 24 hours.

Needless to say, I was stunned. Swade was intent on making this fool's errand an actual thing.

When I asked what he needed from me and the fan community, we kept coming back to Twitter.

The thing about Sungwoo is that during his visit back in August, the whole thing seemed like a homecoming from a family member who just happened to live elsewhere — like meeting a long-lost relative with whom you immediately had a connection. We had to help this family member come back to see his baseball team play in the Fall Classic.

Swade flew the 22 hours to South Korea, and for an entire day, I waited to hear news of what his plans were or even if he was able to meet Sungwoo. And then I got the following email:

> I am in South Korea now (can't sleep) and the prospects of getting SungWoo are looking decent at best. There is a lot of push back from his boss and so far his direct supervisor is even reluctant to take it to the boss who would be the one to give the official okay. The Korean work ethic and culture is what we're up against and they take it very serious.

> SungWoo has been pretty clear that while his co-workers and what he calls "teammates" are incredibly supportive, he is weary of this becoming too big a spectacle where his bosses get the impression he lacks focus on his work. This also happens to be a pretty busy period for the particular department he works in.

> But at the end of the day a groundswell of support in KC and in the States can only help the situation. Who knows maybe someone really key will take notice and open some doors for us over here.

In our original conversation, he admitted that the likelihood of him convincing Sungwoo was pretty good, but convincing his business — the one Sungwoo just started with — to take a week and a half off work, not for the greater good but for himself, was nearly impossible.

So I started to think... what if we could move the needle while telling not just the city, but the world, how important this man is to this community. I sat down and started writing a blog post and sent the following email to Shelov:

> *I'm pretty confident that with the national attention on the Royals right now that we can get #FreeSungWoo trending nationally on Twitter.*

> *The plan is to get the press release from you this afternoon, then release to Danny and Alex around 4:30? At the same*

*time, I"ll push the Pine Tar post. And then we'll see where
it goes...*

At 4:30, Danny Parkins went on the air with a special announcement asking for folks to go to the PineTarPress page and tweet out the (politically corrected) #BringBackSungWoo.

In Twitter parlance, "trending" is a relatively big deal. It is like making the front page of a newspaper or having your name up on a billboard. The formula is a closely guarded secret by Twitter on what becomes "trending" or not, but it includes the number of tweets about a topic or a hashtag and the saturation within a time frame. It also includes whether it's a new phrase; otherwise, Justin Bieber and his 40 million followers would be trending all the time.

That being said, I figured this had a pretty good chance at trending inside of Kansas City very quickly. Instead, #BringBackSungWoo began trending nationally in just under 45 minutes. That means that the hashtag was seen nationwide almost immediately. At its peak, the hashtag was being tweeted about 20 times a second and in total, nearly 20,000 tweets went out with the cry to bring Sungwoo back for the World Series. The tag also trended inside of South Korea for the better part of two days.

We moved the needle, but would it be enough to get Sungwoo back?

It was.

The next morning, the following tweet began making its way around:

It was hardly a confirmed source, but soon after, Shelov and Mag-

Sam Kim 김혜성   Follow
@ghimhehsuhng

@shelovj Rejoice, Josh. Someone at Sungwoo's hotel tells me he's going to Kansas City to watch the @Royals. Sungwoo also confirms it to me.

3:23 AM - 17 Oct 2014

1 RETWEET 2 FAVORITES

gievision confirmed that Sungwoo would, indeed, make it back to Kansas City to watch the World Series.

It's unclear if getting it trending worldwide had any major effect, but the *Wall Street Journal* did write this:

> But with the same kind of bizarro logic that has propelled the Royals' and Mr. Lee's year so far, the improbable suddenly began to look inevitable. (It helped that #bringbacksungwoo became a trending topic on Twitter, a nod to the role that Mr. Lee's Twitter account has played in his public rise.) He got the formal approval on Friday.

The man who, at least partly, helped inspire a city and a baseball team to go past their decades of futility would see them reach the pinnacle of that achievement. Sungwoo would be back for the World Series.

Kansas City in mid-October was in a state of shock. I can only assume what baseball fans in places like New York or St. Louis or San

Francisco feel in March and April when their teams have a respectable shot at a World Series. It simply doesn't happen here in Kansas City. Even with this season being our best shot in years, you couldn't find hardly any national writer or even local blogger or reporter who said they'd get to the World Series. There were many who thought if the right sequence of events happened and you squinted really hard, that the Royals would make the postseason, but if anybody said they would be in the Fall Classic, they were full of shit.

This isn't to say diehard fans weren't hopeful — at some point, though, you can wear the tights and the cape, but you still will never be Superman.

Fountains were dyed blue and banners went up around town, but it was late in the month before Kansas City really realized what was happening. There were high fives and TONS of Royals gear being worn, but the attitude wasn't giddy — it seemed that we were all waiting for the other shoe to drop. Like the NCAA would come in and declare the Royals ineligible and take away our bowl game.

Regardless, the city did eventually start to go nuts about the World Series coming to town and about Games 1 and 2 being here.

Ticket prices were outrageous, and the handling of all postseason tickets by the Royals was a certified train wreck. I watched this from my office as three or four of my friends around me fought with the ticketing website, which would accept your "virtual place in line" and even get so far as to get your credit card information, but then dump you out into the cold blackness of the Internet.

There were reports of this all over the postseason, but eventually, if you wanted in, you found your way in. Kansas Citians might be paying Citibank and Capital One for years, but we got in to see the series. Some paid over a thousand dollars to see the Royals compete in their first World Series since Madonna had a Number 1 hit.

We met Sungwoo at the airport just hours before Game 1 of the World Series. He had his own part to play in the final days of the season. But he would be back with The Committee and his Royals to see this through to the end.

Chapter 19
The Indicator

The 2014 World Series umpiring crew. (left to right) Jerry Meals, Hunter Wendelstedt, Ted Barrett, Jeff Nelson (Crew Chief), Eric Cooper and Jim Reynolds

The name Rick Schmidt isn't a name you would ever know. Rick wanted it that way. Rick was an umpire, and umpires take great pride in knowing that the best umpired games are the ones where they are never noticed. And so it was that most would never know Rick's name. But I knew it, as "Schmitty" was something of a mentor to me — as much as a 30-year umpiring veteran can be a mentor to a 25-year umpiring veteran.

I had a very poignant conversation with Rick several years back as I worked a summer game with him. I asked him to help me with any mechanics or critiques of my game, as he was a long-time veteran of junior college baseball and I hadn't umpired at that level for over a decade.

Rick gave me something of a dressing down about my performance that night. He gave me tips and critiques and busted my ass for about 45 minutes. It ranged from my lack of conditioning to my strike zone to the creases that should've been ironed in my pants.

"You'll never make it at the next level like this," he implored. He delivered it with such care and respect for the game of baseball.

So, I took his advice. I went to extra training. I ironed my pants and shined my shoes, and began to work higher and higher levels of baseball. From there, I worked a number of all-star games, college series and even a championship series in the HAAC.

Rick died that next spring.

He died as all umpires would probably want to die — while walking off the field after a plate job heading back to change between games of a double header. He had a massive heart attack and died within feet of home plate. Nearly all in attendance at the game only knew that "an umpire had a heart attack." Rick would've liked that.

But that's not where the story ends.

The next summer, I was selected to work a summer all-star game of the best college players from around the city. It is a huge honor to be named to that crew, and I had received the even higher honor of being named the plate umpire.

Those of us on that crew wanted to do something to honor Rick, so we had "R.S." embroidered on the side of our hats. We also worked the first pitch of the game without a second base umpire, a "missing man" formation in Rick's honor.

Every umpire carries an "indicator" in his or her left hand. The indicator helps to remind the umpire of the balls, strikes and outs. For higher-level umpires, that indicator is usually a small silver device about the size of a book of matches that fits in your palm. Prior to the game, I bought six new indicators and had them engraved with "Schmitty" on the back. I gave one to each of my three crew members, I kept one and gave the fifth to Rick's family. But the sixth indicator had its own very special, very private story to tell.

The Ban Johnson All Star Game occurred following the Major League game that day in early June. I had arranged to meet the major league umpiring crew that had just finished their game prior to my game. It's always a great honor to meet major league umpires —

they are like meeting members of your favorite band that only a few thousand people know about.

The Ban Johnson league is a summer wood bat only league in the Kansas City area for college kids after their spring seasons are over. It has been operating in the area since 1927, and its MLB alums include Rick Sutcliffe and David Cone.

The day of the all-star game, Tim McClelland was the MLB crew chief. You only know his name because he was the umpire that called the Royals' George Brett out in 1983 during the infamous "Pine Tar Game." The plate umpire that day was Ted Barrett.

Barrett is a pastor when he is not a MLB umpire. He's also a former professional boxer. At 6'4", he would not be my first choice to face off against inside a boxing ring OR a confessional.

Ted was still dripping in sweat following his game when my crew and I entered the umpires' locker room. After exchanging pleasantries and recognizing we had our own game to call, I asked for a moment of silence with both crews of umpires in Rick's name. I then presented Mr. Barrett with the sixth indicator and asked one favor of him — that he use that indicator in a Major League Baseball game. Ted said, "Of course," and we parted ways.

My crew then worked the all-star game. Few things are as special as standing at home plate of Kauffman Stadium calling balls and strikes. This was a memory of a lifetime for me, and it was because of Rick that I was there.

But that's not where the story ends either.

Just four days later, I turned on the television, and on MLB Network they broke in to show the final pitches of a perfect game by Matt Cain, a pitcher for the San Francisco Giants, over the Houston Astros. The announcers, with good reason, praised Cain for throwing his first no-hitter and only the 22nd perfect game in Major League Baseball history. They even went on to praise his catcher and his defense, which was stellar throughout the 27-up-and-27-down performance.

What the announcers, and the fans in the stands, and just about anybody else failed to mention was that the home plate umpire was Ted Barrett. And in his left hand was the silver indicator engraved with "Schmitty." And I also noticed that Ted's shoes were shined and the pleats on his pants were immaculate. Schmitty would've loved that.

Yet that's not where the story ends either.

Jump ahead nearly two years — the Royals went on to sweep both the American League Division Series against the Anaheim Angels and the American League Championship Series against the Baltimore Orioles. The run seemed otherworldly at the time. The club simply clicked where it needed to click, especially with their running game, which stole 14 bases the entire postseason while their opponents stole only four.

The fury and drama of the five-hour Wild Card game seemed to erupt in a shower of adrenaline that led to two weeks of tremendous play from the club. Even Ned Yost seemed to find his groove. After the season, Yost would be quoted saying that he changed how he managed down the stretch, but this season he managed to the team's strengths.

I was watching all of this with giddy excitement. Twenty nine years of longing to see your team succeed in pretty much anything, and then they rattle off eight wins in a row and sweep two series to head to the World Series.

The buzz in the town was at a frenzy. Banners went up downtown overnight. The town was readying for its first World Series in 29 years. And then I got a phone call the day before Game 1 inviting me to a World Series Gala at Kauffman Stadium.

The event was a thank-you to folks who helped with the team, MLB Execs, some off-duty press, key members of the community and me, apparently.

The event was about as swanky as you could get for a stadium that was built in 1969. Ice sculptures, free food, open bar. My kind of party. You could even walk around the warning track as folks descended on the spot Alex Gordon slammed into the fence in ALCS Game 4 only a few nights before.

So I'm walking around Kauffman Stadium only hours before hosting its first World Series game in three decades, and I see six suit-clad men emerge from the stairs. The umpiring crew had stopped in for a quick bite to eat and to check out their surroundings for the next night. Hulking over the other five was Ted Barrett.

My palms began to sweat as I walked up to him and introduced myself again. He didn't recognize me at first until I brought up the indicator. The one with "Schmitty" on the back. His eyes lit up. "OH YES. Do you know what happened to that indicator? The next week I called Cain's perfect game!" Um. Yeah. I was aware.

There were four umpires on that crew working their first World Series. Eric Cooper, Jerry Meals, Hunter Wendelstedt and Jim Reynolds all would be stepping onto a World Series field for the first time. Wendelstedt and Reynolds were both classmates of mine in the early 1990s when I went to professional umpire school. That seems like 50 years ago, yet here we were shaking hands before the city's big night.

For Barrett, this was his third World Series. When I asked him if he was nervous, he admitted that he gets "excited."

"Hey. Give me your address. I've been hoping to run into you again. I want to give that indicator back to you."

Umpires are often called many things — most of them bad. The old saying goes if you know an umpire's name, they've done a bad job. But I will never forget the names Ted Barrett and Rick Schmidt.

Chapter 20

The Ending

Sungwoo, in his apartment in Seoul, South Korea, celebrates the Royals clinching a post-season berth for the first time in 29 years

Just before Game 6 of the World Series, I got a text from Alex. He's my friend that works for MLB.com. The Royals were trailing the San Francisco Giants 3-2 in the series, and the games were heading back to Kansas City. But Kansas City was facing elimination for the first time in October. The text read, "We need to do something about this."

"We need to take matters into our own hands," I replied, knowing where this was leading, yet not wanting to be the guy who asked his buddy for a ticket to the World Series. So I played along.

"We need to get the band back together."

Alex was referring to the rhythm and blues review squad of Dr. Jazayerli, Alex's dad, Alex and myself. The "band" was 1-0 in witnessing life-altering baseball games together and, as mentioned above, there were elements of the paranormal at play that simply could not be danced around.

"Meet me at Gate C tomorrow by 5. You will have a ticket to the World Series."

"I'll see if I can work it into my schedule." (Then I did the Willie Mays Hayes dance from *Major League*.)

Oh, Jake Peavy. You poor, poor bastard. You never knew what hit you. It wasn't your sore thumb, which you were complaining about prior to the baseball game. It was the Wild Card Wizards. (We really need to pick a name, because that one is awful.) You can blame the five runs you gave up in the second inning only on Rany, Alex, Alex's dad and me. Sorry, man. You tried.

We were now a force to be reckoned with. We had twice staved off elimination of our favorite baseball team.

The entire night, there was the same sense that I remember from 1985. From the first pitch it was clear that the Giants had no shot — just like Game 7 against the Cardinals. This was our game. This was our moment. This was our year.

Our ace in the hole for all the games of the World Series, obviously, was Lee Sungwoo. Back from South Korea to see the team of destiny.

When he was here in August, he saw a streak of victories — three of them against the San Francisco Giants. The mojo was real, and it was unstoppable.

The only problem was... we peaked a game too early. Here's where it all started to break down.

Following Game 6, Alex simply turned to me and said, "Well, we have to come back." So back we came for Game 7.

Many of you were there and many of you already know the story. And, frankly, it still makes me a little sick to my stomach. But you know the gist. The Royals dropped in the hole early, then tied it up, then fell behind by one. Then Gordon's single with a two-base error, putting him on third in the ninth.

Then the silence.

It is this silence that I keep coming back to. We're all still numb. I can't even tell you what the Chiefs' record was this year. Missouri football went to a bowl game, but it was all white noise to keep me from the silence. Ninety feet away.

This silence really hit me the next day and several days after that when I went through a bit of a mild depression. I was down. I was mad. Mad at everything.

I was mad at god damn Salvador Perez, who swung at a pitch in his eyes.

I was mad at Maggievision and ESPN and MLB for taking up so much of Sungwoo's time schmoozing with Paul Rudd that I don't think he got to watch much of the World Series.

I was mad at the Royals for pulling my press credential to the Wild Card game, killing my chances of seeing a postseason game from the press box.

I was mad at Mike Jirschele for holding up Alex Gordon at third — forever keeping him one base away from tying the game in the ninth.

I was mad at Joe Buck and Hunter Pence and Madison Bumgarner.

I didn't want it to end. But painfully I was forced to watch it end as Pablo Sandoval clutched the final out of the World Series.

But the silence also allows you to bring things into focus, just as it did on that beach for me a few years ago. My silence opened up a vein of creativity that bled into my writings and my Twitter account and my work. My silence allowed me to write this little book and interact with people from across the globe.

There was no reason to be mad at Salvador Perez. He had caught over 150 games that season. He's a free swinger. Ned Yost was never, in a million years, going to pinch hit for him in that situation, and the last time he was up to end a game, he won the damn thing on a pitch that was even worse.

Maggievision played a hunch. There's no reason to get mad at them. They worked with MLB and ESPN to make a dream come true for Sungwoo, just as we had nudged him in August. The World Series is a well-orchestrated event, however, and the price he paid for free World Series tickets and airfare was to sit next to Kansas City-born actor Paul Rudd. You could do much worse.

We didn't get a ton of time with Sungwoo on his second trip to the United States in three months, but that made the time we did get to spend with him — in his hotel room a couple times and at a pizza parlor for Game 3, after closing down a bar for Game 2 — all the more special. He's an incredible guy, and he has seen some incredible things over the last few months.

The Royals press box fits less than 50 people. Over 300 credentials were requested, and I'm guessing a guy with a Twitter handle of "Fake Ned" was at the bottom of the pile. Plus, I got to watch every World Series game anyway.

Mike Jirschele began his minor league managing career in 1992. He managed in the minors for over 20 years, and this was his first season with the Major League ballclub. He's seen more baseball games than you could ever wish to see in your life. He held up Alex Gordon because Alex Gordon would've been out by 35 feet. Gordon left the batter's box never thinking he'd end up on third, and he never should have. There were three bobbles made on that play, and the throw was still in the relay man's hand when Gordon was a step off of third. Mike Jirschele made the right decision.

Fox Sports announcer Joe Buck is a tool. I totally nailed that one. But Hunter Pence and Madison Bumgarner actually seem like pretty nice guys.

The great baseball movie *Bull Durham* has a quote about baseball. It's actually making fun of baseball clichés by coming up with the most perfect baseball cliché, and it goes like this:

"This is a very simple game. You throw the ball, you catch the ball, you hit the ball. Sometimes you win, sometimes you lose, sometimes it rains."

Sometimes the game ends, and sometimes you lose.

Lee Sungwoo, Dave Darby, Rany Jazayerli, Chris Kamler, and Brett Kamler reflect on the World Series (photo by Lee Sungwoo)

Chapter 21

The End

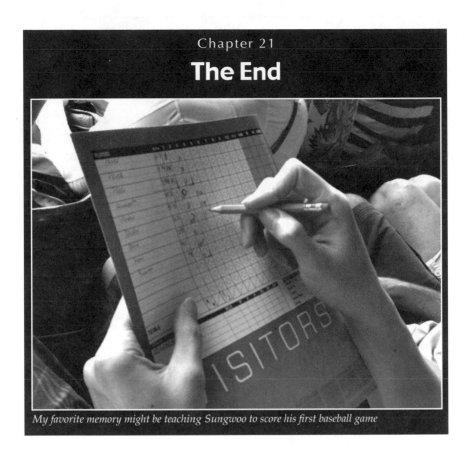

My favorite memory might be teaching Sungwoo to score his first baseball game

When I was a little boy, I grew up on the east side of Kansas City in the shadow of East High School. We moved to the Northland when I was five, but my earliest memories are of the orange shag carpeting that was all the rage in the mid-1970s.

This was before my other brother and sisters were more than just toddlers, so I remember this brick A-frame house on Van Brunt as MY house. I had a bedroom to myself. Sliding down the steps on my butt was my own personal invention. My Evel Knievel Big Wheel terrorized the sidewalks of my neighborhood. And my backyard was my Royals stadium.

The tools of the trade were simple, yet elegant. The white dimpled wiffle ball, the orange super-sized plastic bat and a beer flat as home plate. My father threw enough batting practice to throw out a rotator cuff and necessitate Tommy John surgery. The scene was always the same.

Bottom of the ninth. Winning run steps to the plate. Game Seven of the World Series.

My dreams were like those of millions of boys of that generation, but those boys all melted away to this singular moment in my backyard. Goose Gossage on the mound. Chris Kamler at the plate.

Here's the pitch.

As I remember it, every swing was grand and belted the white ball over the arched two-story roof into the front yard. Every time.

Of course, as you grow older, those perfect memories sour a bit. As I got older and we moved north, I realized that not every swing ends in a towering home run onto the grass slope in left field. Not every connection is square.

Another great baseball cliché is that "the hardest thing to do in sports is hit a round ball with a round bat." Others are that "baseball is a game in which failing seven out of ten times puts you in the Hall of Fame" and "a pitcher who gives up three runs or less each game will likely win a Cy Young."

You learn all of these things after you get out of the backyard. After your parents move away from your friends. After you realize that butt-sliding down the stairs isn't the best for your footie pajamas.

Life lessons wrapped into the stitches of a baseball. It's not until later in life you learn about the silence.

When we moved to the house I grew up in, I shared a room with my little brother. He and I had a relatively traditional hate-hate relationship as bunkbed roommates. About the same time, I was sitting on the floor, now deep brown shag carpeting, watching the 1976 American League Championship series. Chris Chambliss hit a towering home run to win the series, and I saw the iconic image of fans rushing the field. But in my head I heard only silence.

The iconic image the next morning in the *Kansas City Times* was of my favorite shortstop Freddie Patek cradling his head in his hands in the dugout. Weeping. The picture was filled with the silence of baseball. For every winner, there is a loser.

Hitting wiffle balls in the backyard yields to video games and band practice and learning that your baseball career ends at age 14. You also learn that life is a series of failures surrounded by moments of glee and bliss. But you learn to survive the failure because those Royals, who lost three years straight to the Yankees, finally swept them in 1980. Perseverance through the silence.

The story of Game 7, October 29, 2014, is all about where you are in your own personal journey with the silence. Many will see Salvador Perez popping out weakly on a Madison Bumgarner eyebrow burner as a failure and allow themselves to be swallowed by the silence. They'll see it as a brief blip in 29 years of futility. They'll see that waiting for Dayton Moore's process was ultimately unsuccessful.

Then there will be those of us for whom what we saw punctured through the silence like a scream in church.

We'll remember where it all started, when the jetliner touched down at KCI and we took a chance on a man who took a chance on us. A man we didn't even know could speak English.

We'll remember ground zero, when the franchise shed the shackles of 29 years of abominable baseball: cutoff throws hitting people in the back; outfielders jumping against a wall, only for the ball to land in front of them; Eduardo Villacis and Brian Anderson. We'll remember the day it ended. The day he hung the W.

We'll remember what he left us with — the winning streak, the smiles and the Postseason.

But most of all I'll remember that the silence after the series wouldn't have happened without the season of Sungwoo.

In the end, the Royals didn't win the World Series. I was actually toying around with the idea of writing this chapter as if they did. Talk about the parade with Sungwoo in the lead car. Talk about the fourth and final champagne celebration. Talk about the embrace between Sungwoo and Ned Yost on the mound following the game.

Photo courtesy Lee Sungwoo

Granted. It was an early draft of an idea and I had had a couple of drinks.

But I think it turned out just the way it needed to turn out. The end of this story isn't written yet. The 2015 Royals have more work to do. Sungwoo has more work to do. We all have more work to do as fans and as Kansas Citians.

We had a helluva party for three months here in Kansas City, but it's a town still suffering from the 29 years of losing and now 30 years since winning a World Series. There is another chapter waiting to be written, perhaps by my son, when he too begins to gray around the temples, like his dad.

The Beatles said it best when they said, "In the end, the love you take is equal to the love you make," and that's a perfect way to see the 2014 baseball season. The cheering. The crowds. The stranger hugs. The crime going down in the city. All of the love this town showed this humble man from South Korea. The love he shot right back. The cup overfloweth with memories, and 90 feet isn't going to take that away from anybody.

Sungwoo leads a World Series rally at Power & Light District in Kansas City (Photo from Dave Darby)

Epilogue by Lee Sungwoo

Sungwoo and Jimmy Faseler celebrate a Royals victory (photo by Lee Sungwoo)

The silence. Only keyboard typing noise is here at work, all team-mates are tied up with project for Incheon Int'l airport duty free store concession these days. My phone is buzzing. Twitter notification. A faint smile with familiar names. So boring offseason, please come back soon baseball!! For a moment, my mind wanders and leads me to that night. Game 7.

Nobody walked up to me, no one talked to me. I was sitting alone in silence right behind glass door in the George Brett Suite. My face was dark with tight lips. Once after Royals trailed by Michael Morse's RBI single off Kelvin Herrera in the 4th, I couldn't stay out there with fans and cameras of MaggieVision's 30 for 30 team. I could not hide my impatient, relentless, anxious, uneasy look.

DANG it!! Bad hunch proved to be true all the time. I was seized by ominous feeling as soon as an idea came to mind that Yost might stick with Guthrie too long after he ended a nice 1-2-3 inning in 3rd.

Giants "MadBum" came back to pitch on just two days' rest in the 5th inning and Infante greeted him with a leadoff single, but Royals couldn't bring him home, then next 14 batters retired.

But with two outs in the ninth, Gordon's hit to left-center was missed by center fielder Gregor Blanco and then left fielder Juan Perez dropped the ball that put Gordon at third base. I stamped my feet and clapped my sweaty hands together. Next batter was injured Salvador Perez, who hit a homer from Bumgarner in Game 1 & a walk-off single in the Wild Card Game against the A's, but he got Salvy with foul out. An air of silence filled the house.

That night I couldn't sleep much, turned over from one side to the other. Spacious hotel room was a completely desolated island. Silence was all over the place. Greeted dawn while I exchanged text messages and Skyped with mom, another diehard Royals fan in Korea my brother and wife. The pain in their voice showed me enough how upset they were too.

Before I left for Royals Fan Rally at The K, there was short final interview with 30 for 30 team Josh and Anthony. With sleepless dull head, it was total disastrous rambling with my broken English. Now I don't even remember what questions & answers all about at all.

But in the end, they asked me for a farewell speech in Korean. Free from Englishphobia, I was a bit loosened up. At that very moment, lost control of my emotions. Eyes were wet with tears, my voice was shake. Quickly I turned away my eyes. The producer Josh Swade wiped his tears behind camera. We were silent as we realized this is it, time to say good bye.

The scene printed on my memory is the Royals Fan Rally.

I left the hotel room with a heavy heart. Not sure I was ready to face other fans & players. No idea what it would look like, just a day after Royals suffered a heartbreaking loss in Game 7 of the World Series.

But once I got to The K, thousands of fans packed Kauffman Stadium. They showed up to thank to players and to celebrate the team's memorable postseason. It was another perfect way for me to remember "Midwest hospitality" How warm hearted, how generous, how wonderful people of Kansas City are.

Thank you so much. For everything.

"It was a great season," I keep talking to myself. I'm so proud of my Royals players, coaches, franchise members and Kansas City people. I am blessed to be there in KC to be a part of this remarkable season for entire my life.

And I believe it's just the beginning of a journey to bring back a World Championship to the city, then #BringBackSungWoo one more time!!

Lee Sungwoo
January, 2015

Lee Sungwoo reflects on his trips to Kansas City following the 2014 World Series at the postseason rally, (Photo courtesy Josh Shelov)

KICKSTARTER BACKERS

Adam Cooper

Chris Atkins

Taylor McConville

John Craig

Alex Thompson

Steve

Brett Taylor

Kyle Beger

Stephanie Fields

Darren Papek

Phillip Crow

Paul O'Neill

Eric Kegley

Jason Conley

Brian Walker

Nathan Saper

Tate Cristgen

Jason Sherer

Jeff Dunlap

Colleen Harding

Gracey Terrill

Cody Kirschner

Andrea Kindvall

Trudy Martin

Mary Beth Hedlund

Jeremy Zimmerli

Wayne Wollesen

Shari Creason

Gene Winters

Chad Rohr

Denise Cross

John Erik Pattison

Alex Rovinson

Will Ruder

Kristina Fulk

Chad King

Seth Meadows

Danny Ritz

Josh Harrold

John Heath

Joe Accurso

Becky Roberts

Brad Bowers

Bob and Jan Atkins

Dave Smith

Dan Johnston

Amy Ogden Steelman

Shannon

Aimee Patton

Nathaniel Green

Zach and Jenny

Denise Malan

Geoff Gerling

Matt Wormus

Roger Erickson

Lindsay

Mark McCombs

Mary Gulick

KICKSTARTER BACKERS

Carl DeAmaral

April Veale

Mary Blakley

Aaron

Justin Parker

Bob Rippy

Cathy Fulks

Kandy Jones Hartzell

Michael Mahoney

Natalie Guthrie Johnson

Jeff Orth

Brent Snyder

Gregg Glass

Erin Bradstreet

Brian Joe

Jay Regan

Derek Ramsay

Dalia Vargas

Sandra Hedlung Tunnell

Elizabeth Belden

Craig Little

Bryan Sexton

Scott Kramer

Mike Bransfield

Kristi Cavansugh

Kyle Ritchie

Jenny Raynor

Mark Ferguson

Tyler Hillsman

Michael Jacobi

Anna Weber

Eric Wright

Todd Barton

Noah Cundiff

Michael Lewis

Luke Chandler

Jeff Wayman

Vicki Jones

Tom Hand

CaptainLatte

Dave Darby

Michael Engel

Johny Barnett

Shannon Shelton

Ryan McNellis

Josh Mortensen

Jason Boster

Shannon Peterson

Ivan Foley

Kelly Kirkpatrick

Steve Cosentino

Zach Holden

Acknowledgements

I never thought I would write a book. I never thought I would write... well... anything, really. My canvas was Twitter's 140 characters at a time. This was WAY out of my comfort zone. So please understand when I say that I could not have done it without you. Yes, you — and those of you who helped Kickstart the book and the ones who followed me on Twitter or read my columns in the *Platte County Landmark* or visited my blog.

This is your fault... er... you made this possible.

I want to thank my wife Kara and son Brett for putting up with my crazy shenanigans and coming along on as many of them as you did. To my son Andrew — you were there through all of it.

To those of you who helped with editing, Brett Dufur and Zach Hively as well as Molly McMurtrey, Michael Engel, and David Lesky, thank you. My writing style is... unorthodox. So thanks for bending around it. Special shout out to Brett who also helped save my life. So. I guess I owe you two now.

Thanks to Chris Wheelhouse for calling me every day in December asking if the book was done yet, and if not, why not. It's not my fault you don't know what humor is. But you do know what being a great friend is, and I'll never be able to repay you.

I do want to recognize the tremendous Kickstarter backers who helped make this book a reality. Early after the first draft of the book, I went to go print it out at a Kinkos and it all became very real. It was as if I was holding the past three months of my life in my hand. You did that. You helped make this. And now it's a book. An honest-to-God book. Thank you.

I want to thank everyone associated with the Kansas City Royals for their tremendous support with Sungwoo's visit. I haven't always been a good fan. In fact, I've been a pain in your ass. You were the bigger man and I appreciate it. I also want to thank every business, franchise and selka-asker who helped out, as well. ("Selka" is Korean for "selfie.")

The first two chapters tell a bit of my personal journey from over the past two years — it is through this process you really learn who your best friends are. But thank you. I love you all very much.

I'd also like to thank "The Welcoming Committee," and especially Dave Darby, Ethan Bryan, and Elizabeth Belden, for putting up with my special brand of complexity. This wouldn't have been nearly what it was without you.

Mom. Dad. Aunts. Uncles. Brother. Sisters. Sally Field, Ivan Foley and my high school English teacher, Mrs. Jones — this book is for you as well.

Finally, I want to thank Lee Sungwoo. There are no words, even though I've tried to write many here. You're an inspiration.

Photo Credits

Unless specified in the caption, all photographs were taken by the author. You can go to *kamlerbook.com* to see full color pictures and photos that didn't make it into the book.

Other Credits

The chapter "The Indicator" contains content originally produced for *Referee* magazine in a story called "Last Call: An Indicator of Respect" by Chris Kamler from the May 2014 edition. Reprinted with written permission from *Referee* magazine. For subscription information, contact *Referee* magazine at (800) 733-6100 or www.referee.com.

Portions of several passages in the book were posted previously at pinetarpress.com and ramblingmorons.com. They have been reprinted with permission.

Additional portions of the book were printed previously in *The Platte County [MO] Landmark* newspaper. They have been reprinted with permission. Subscriptions to *The Landmark* are available at plattecountylandmark.com

All Major League Baseball logos and trademarks appearing in text and photographs, including the Kansas City Royals, Postseason logo, World Series logo and any other logos and trademark from MLB teams including the MLB logo are used within fair use rights.

All tweets and images embedded within tweets including the Twitter™ logo are used within fair use rights.

About the Author

Chris Kamler is a lifelong Kansas Citian and tortured sports fan. He is also a freelance journalist, author and broadcaster. He has a weekly column called "The Rambling Moron" in *The Platte County Landmark*, and he is the editor of TheKCPost.com.

Chris has contributed content to Sports Radio 810, ESPN 1510, 810Varsity.com, PineTarPress.com and *Referee Magazine*.

In his spare time, Chris is the voice behind the widely panned @TheFakeNed Twitter account. Additionally, he is the creator and host of the UmpTalk podcast at umptalk.com.

Chris has a wife and two children and lives in Kansas City North. You can reach him through his Twitter @ChrisKamler or on Facebook.com/chriskamler or at chriskamler.com